Peachey Letters

Love Letters to Life

Or how to...
question, celebrate and live life to the full!

Sandra Peachey

Peachey Letters

First published in 2013 by Anoma Press Ltd

48 St Vincent Drive, St Albans, Herts, AL1 5SJ UK

info@anomapress.com

www.anomapress.com

Book layout by Charlotte Mouncey

Printed on acid-free paper from managed forests. This book is printed on demand to fulfill orders, so no copies will be remaindered or pulped.

ISBN 978-1-908746-71-9

Dedicated to my mother:

Agnes Peachey

Who was born in 1926 and died in 2012 - during
the writing of this book and who has,
for many reasons,
been my greatest teacher...

May all be known; may all be right;
may all be good; may all be realised...

~ *Sandra Peachey*

ACKNOWLEDGEMENTS

This book is a compound of so many people, influences, memories and processes that I couldn't possibly do justice to them all in a few short paragraphs (or even many long ones come to think of it...).

Firstly, my biggest thanks must go to the recipients of each of these letters, both named and unnamed – you have all been my inspiration and have moved me towards the realisation of the dream to be published, so my gratitude can really know no bounds for that.

I have to express my huge appreciation to everyone who commented on the Letters in my Blog before it was published on paper - via all the social media platforms, as well as on the blog itself: www.peacheyletters.co.uk. Your positive observations have spurred me on to turn a Blog into a Book – this Peachey tome would, quite simply, not exist without you.

To all the family, friends, colleagues and cohorts – living and departed, who have supported me and my dreams, through your thoughts, words and deeds - I acknowledge my love and deep debt. You know who you all are, and I want you to know too, that this book is my loving homage to you.

To all the 'book people' who have coached, edited, financed, published, PR'ed and advised me – thus enabling these words to become print; I am thankful for and prize your belief, expertise and input so very much.

And so it is, that this book is a true team product – a universal effort which goes way beyond the mentioning of individual names - so, once again – *thank you all.*

Sandra Peachey

The Response to the Peachey Letters Blog

This collection of letters started life as a blog in 2012. With January of that year fast passing me by, I set myself the creative challenge of writing a love letter to life – every day of the Valentine month of February. From the moment the first letter went live, I was genuinely amazed by the response that the letters received and here follows just *some* of the huge volume of feedback that my blog has garnered ...

www.peacheyletters.co.uk... the feedback...

Wow, that letter to your father is so touching. Brave writing Sandie.

~ Susan Brookes

Sandie this letter to your Dad is so beautiful I cried... I thank you for your wonderful open-hearted letter...

~ Kay Kirkby

Beautiful Sandra, just awesome.

~ Nadine Honeybone

I shouldn't have read that, I now have a wet face... My dad... I love him dearly and this beautiful letter is a reminder of all of the good stuff to be treasured. Thank you – blubbering of South Wales.

~ Jacqui Malpass

Wow, what a wonderful letter to your Dad, Sandie. I last wrote to my Dad a couple of years before he died... I've had a bit of a blubbery morning of it so far (good stuff!) so thank you! Blubbering of Cambridge (wonder if that means I'm related to Blubbering of South Wales!)

~ Diana Barden

That is such a beautiful letter to your Dad, Sandie – made me shed a few tears...

~ Sue Balcon

Wow, Sandie, that [Letter to My Father] is fabulous, and I love that picture of the two of you together, such a picture of a strong man, giving you the support to be you!

~ Sue Maggott

Sandie, you brought me to tears. Such beautiful letters from a beautiful woman.

~ Deborah Meredith

Gorgeous gorgeous gorgeous – thank you for sharing Sandie, such a beautiful idea, these letters will make an amazing book.

~ Michelle Clarke

What a wonderful thing to do, very touching and very real.

~ Lisa Hayward

A fabulous idea and wonderful share Sandie – bless you.

~ Joanna McCormick

What a fab idea. It brought tears to my eyes too. It also made me realise that I should write letters to my parents too while they are here to read them. Thanks for sharing, you are a wonderful writer, I look forward to reading the next one!

~ Lyn Bromley

I really love this message Sandra [Letter to my Father].

~ Richard Wilkins

An amazing process to go through Sandie, and very powerful letters.

~ Sue Maggott

Thanks for the letter and all the effort you put into your relationships. You are a true friend.

~ Susan Tarney

Your letters are brilliant. What an amazing talent you have.

~ Hayley Wilkins

Wow. I love this letter [to Every Woman]. *Thank you for taking the time to put this in writing so beautifully. Every woman on the planet should read it.*

~ Alex Santaro-Emmerson

How many emotions you pass on to me through this letter [To my Mother]*; smiles at you being hauled up in front of the – Head AKA Care Manager of the Home; tears when you mention your Mum's broken childhood and then 'all those dark words were not really you'; relief and joy for you when you describe the love creating a force field around you.*

The honesty, not ducking the hard parts, make it so much more real as a love letter... everyone has their darker moments or the things that are difficult to say to someone so close as a mother. I really smiled when you mentioned your 'Karma' to Arthur – it's a lovely way to see it. In fact the whole letter is so beautifully written, I can see how you're able to help so many others on a very deep level. You do have a precious gift.

What a gift that is – coming through all your life and coming to this point of deep peace and love. And you've had the honesty to share it. I just feel so touched and humbled. Thank you with all my heart.

~ Lyria Normington

Thank you for sharing your letters with us all. You have such a wonderful gift with words.

~ Monique Blackmore

I am loving your letters Sandie – you write beautifully with wisdom and grace. Thank you for the acknowledgement [Letter to Every Woman] *– which says so much about the gorgeous goddess that you are. We are all blessed with your writing, your love & your courage.*

~ Lucie Bradbury

[Letter to Lucie Bradbury] *I love it – it's beautiful, it's so you. I had to stop half way through to recover from the tears (tears are good!). A few points felt brutal to read – but then I know love and truth go hand in hand. I am so honoured and grateful that you would write to me (and appreciate too that you have graciously asked for my approval before going public).*

~ Lucie Bradbury

Thank you sooooo much for your beautiful letter and for your love, it's fabulous the way you are able to express your feelings with sensitivity and humour, a real talent.

Just re-read your lovely letter to me and Richard [Letter to the Rocket Man and the Bonny Wee Lass] *and I just wanted to tell you once again how much it means to us both... your writing is so wonderfully poetic whilst at the same time being merrily mischievous, just like you... really feel you could create a beautiful book with all of these when February is finished... I'd buy your first copy.*

~ Liz Ivory

11

I have commented on a few of your letters already, but wanted to tell you, I have found them really moving and I feel like I have got to know you better through them too. I really think you have a career as a writer – or at least as part of your strategy – you write beautifully. Well done for committing and sticking to your promise! You have also inspired me to write some letters... So thank you for inspiring me Sandie. I am sure you have inspired many more.

~ Lyn Bromley

[Letter to Money] *My heart's opened. What a beautiful thing you are doing!!!!!*

~ Sarupa Shah

Sandra, thank you. Your letters are touching and inspirational – and so amazingly well written, they made my spine tingle...

~ Lis Protherough

Wonderful memories that made my eyes leak, a lot! Thank you for reminding me of my own Dad, and Mum, both long gone but never forgotten.

~ Greg C

Rarely have I read such exquisite passion, such positivity, such zest for life as I have in your love letters. You express yourself so well, as you find just the right words for thoughts, feelings and experiences that so many of us find impossible to capture, or even know exist. You have THE GIFT. The gift of self expression. And you have imagination too. A mind able to fly and to dream. To truly know, to see in your mind's eye, how beautiful things could be... if only... Yet, even in this imperfect world... a world fall of faults, pain, failings, evil and just plain indifference, you still see and appreciate the beauty. The beauty that most of us miss as we hurry along the road, immersed in our thoughts about later... or before... the past, or the future... never the now!

You're clearly a woman of many facets, each revealed like a sparkling ray of light as it passes through a crystal... Not just any crystal, but a diamond. A diamond's beauty is revealed through the working of the stone. Life has done its work on you, shaping you through both the pleasure and the pain. The beauty was always there, as it is in all of us, but it doesn't shine out from all of us. In choosing to shine, you give the rest of us permission to shine also. Permission to cast off that which does not serve us and to embrace true joy, through deciding to follow our hearts and our passion.

~ David W

Dear Sandra/Sandie, Most of us if not all get a defining moment in life. That powerful momentary permutation. My moment was when I read your beautiful letters today. What vivid pictures your words paint. It is never easy to put your feelings into words. Your deep feelings and gut reactions bubble up naturally seemingly beyond translation. Your words have become the sparkle in my eyes and the sun that shines through the window every morning beckoning me to wake, I love your writing. I always have, and I always will.

~ Vaibhav – Mumbai, India

[Letter to Loss]. *A heartfelt letter beautifully written.*

~ Lindsay Burton

[Letter to Daftness]. *Made me laugh – love your daftness and your love.*

~ Gill Potter

[Letter to Loss]. *This is truly beautiful. Thank you for sharing your thoughts.*

~ Mary Joyce

Just read your 'To Celebration' letter and frankly I am amazed!! Where have you been hiding this talent??

~ Keith Higham

Wow! Beyond words, your writing is wonderful, your insights an inspiration, the gift of a goddess and an honesty that is humbling... Your bravery is bold and simply brilliant. Thank you.

~ Lucie Bradbury

Awesome Sandra and my heart and love go out to you. Your letter [To Loss] *helped me move on from something too... 'it was as it was meant to be'... so thank you from the bottom of my heart.*

~ Nadine Honeybourne

Very moving, sending you love and thank you for sharing this.

~ Harriet Stack

Wow – so beautiful, thank you Sandie – it connected with me on so many levels [Letter to Loss].

~ Anne Mulliner

CONTENTS

A PEACHEY INTRODUCTION

Disquisition on a Peach

You have a Peach in your hand... I will let *you* decide if this is a literal or a literary peach...

Balanced in the hand, it has a pleasing weightiness, and is comprised of a gorgeous mass – combined and composed of stone, flesh, juice and skin... Bring it up to your nose and you inhale an exotic elixir of aroma and promise, so that your mouth starts to water in glorious anticipation of what is offered within. Within that velvet-like skin, tickling your touch sense, as you trace the curves and ample dimples and then, oddly, you see a straight crease, tracing from tip to base of this abundance of nature; this fuzzy fantasy of fruity covering is coloured in ripe hues of darkened redness, spreading into classic peachy orangeness, through to creamy yellow lightness...

Slice into the giving gorgeous flesh and already it oozes onto and juices your knife. Trace the knife around the hard, hidden stone, forbidding you to go further, then twist the flesh and the peach squelches apart, a half in each hand. Juice runs from the dissected flesh and onto your plate, spilled to be forgotten or maybe to be later lovingly licked. One half of the peach holds a stone, bearing the succulence of clinging fleshy sinews. The stone is purpled and pitted and still partly hidden in its protective half, whilst the opposite piece of peach bears the perfect, pitted indentation of the very heart of the fruit... the potential seed, generations of tree, blossom and fruit, seldom seen, yet nestled in a cool protective womb within.

And the flesh anticipates you – it is luscious and fragrant; its giving succulent firmness coloured steadily and evenly all the way through with a dreamy, salacious creamy orangey tint. The fruity flesh is of fibre and water made – solid yet giving compacted deliciousness, which the teeth can scrape or sink into: to devour, to divine, to taste... And the juice is unleashed and unbound and runs down the fruit and threatens sticky hands and stained clothes – potentially to be spilled... un-tasted and wasted.

And will you feel the neutral tang of the downy skin on the tongue or instead peel away this fuzzy protection? All this attention to get to the taste, to the juice: to be satisfied and slaked, and the taste – now it is here – is *divine*: made of sunshine, of ripeness, of perfumed glorious atoms.

And this is the structure and complexity of a Peach – of the seen and unseen, of the peeling away and the savouring. And so it is that all Peaches are made up of stone, flesh, juice and skin, each component serving their purpose and all fulfilled in some way, shape or fruity form.

So the Peach is lovingly described by *me*: a creation with a Peachey name; then so too shall this fruity device form the structure of this book – my lexicon of love in letters.

As my letters are a journey, so too has my fruity namesake been on a long voyage through the world. The peach originated as a native fruit of China. Then it left that land and the fruit and the word for it has evolved and travelled through the centuries. On its arrival in Britain it first had to borrow the Latin naming of 'malum persicum' – literally the 'Persian apple'; then the Norman conquerors of the British Isles trans-morphed this noun into the sibilant French 'pêche'; and then again, the fruit's name solidified into the harder sounding 'peach' in the Middle English speech of my long ago forebears.

Idle curiosity and a little light research into my surname revealed the phenomena of the peach as a noun, with one of its ancient meanings being 'sinful one'. This noun naming vibrates the fruit and my name with shades and tastes of Eve and the Apple: a thing both wicked and delicious; a forbidden fruit – wanton, wanted, then plucked and devoured. Once gorged, the deliciousness gave way to rottenness and all was changed in the Garden of Eden.

And now in colloquial American English, being 'peachy' has a whole lighter, happier meaning – of being fine, of feeling great; a meaning that has sailed back over the Atlantic to add to the melange of meaning. And so both the sin and the sunshine elements of my surname combine… as they come together, so often, in my letters.

A Peachey Life, in Letters...

When I set myself the creative challenge of writing at least twenty-nine *'Love Letters to Life'* in February 2012, I only knew that I was starting out on a journey and was not even sure where the destination was... More it was something I felt compelled to do – that I had a deep sense of wanting to express my creativity in writing and give gratitude for an amazing life. And since starting the letters I have explored emotions, tackled many issues in my life, mused on the trivial and the poignant (for ME that is...) and delved into my past, present and future, finding a huge catharsis, quite unintentionally, along the way.

And unbidden, the topics of my life came out to play: the people, the phenomena, the passions and professions... Then as I received more and more positive feedback from so many people, the letters felt and shared with me their own logic, and found their own recurring themes, so I could make sense of myself and then share my own brand of wisdom – my life's lessons, encapsulated in my Peachey Letters. And thus the book was born, and had formed itself, and was waiting for me to sift and shape it.

And sometimes it was painful and sometimes it was confusing to air these issues, these feelings. Then again it was liberating and joyful too and the writer in me wanted this creative outlet, to have free reign, to find her own voice and her own way. So what at first seemed to be free flowing and anarchical, found its own structure and logic along the way.

So a book was born. It was an unplanned baby, yet such a gratefully received gift. Somewhere or other it is stated that everyone has a book in them; and over my lifetime, so many plots have swirled through my childish and adult consciousness and asked to be given life: in my fantasies these dreamed out fictional plots would form themselves easily into fame, and yet were never completed or committed to paper.

Now here my first book is, and it seems that it wrote itself, quite easily, with my gentle support. Instead of fiction it seems strange that it is MY story, my stories – forming themselves into this first published long piece of work. Though they are based on solid reality, they are too my own internalised perceptions, my versions, my knowings, my slantings, a work indeed of self fictionalised fact.

The Anatomy of a Peach and of a Peachey...

As they were written, each letter had its own life, its own purpose and momentum. Yet they all had one thing in common – they are all products of this Peachey life and so it was that the device and description of a *peach*, drew them together into one, solid volume.

So letters become book, and introductions and elucidations are called for ... I will wrap each chapter within my peach-like structure – the players and phenomena therein and how they play their part in my simple Peachey philosophies.

So each chapter will, in every sense be a *fruition*, a gathering together of letters around a theme, and each fruitful component will explain and combine the co-existing elements contained therein.

Each element shall play its part: shall gather all together; be a container for all the possible purposes of the letters... Be that to engage, to entertain, to illuminate; and still to share my simple Peachey philosophies: to open windows on my life, my own scribed stories, so that they may resonate and grow their own fruit too, in those who open the letters and read, devour, savour and digest them.

And if a letter strikes a chord with you, take note... are there issues there for you too? That chord could be harmonious or it could be discordant. Think of how you too can celebrate, elucidate, learn and either love or let go of whatever that chiming chord is?

Upon reading my letters, many people have felt moved to write their own. So if you feel moved to make your own love letters: take action and *do* write, do speak, do tell... share, unburden, analyse and always celebrate. Start a journal, start a blog, start a conversation... simply begin and then see where that journey takes you. I cannot promise you that the route is always an easy one, yet I know that for *me*, I love the destination, with its completeness and contentment. A destination where I am freer, I know more, I feel expanded and where I have communicated and connected with like-hearted souls – be they an audience of one or of many or simply the scratch of pen on paper – seen only by me. It is the act of sharing that is vital. So simply share your 'letters' in whatever way you will.

As a coach – someone who supports people in having the life, work and businesses they want, it all has to start with me. I have to do the work, shake things up, settle them down and then move on from them, so that I can help others to do the very same. This journey through life is about learning our own lessons and lovingly living with them; and also, so often, moving on from them. By creating these Peachey Letters I have, in so many ways, become my own best coach.

And as the reader, what, I wonder will be *your* own coaching creation?

So here it is that the beginning ends. It is time now to open up the 'fruit', cut into its flesh and reveal what lies within.

Letter to the World

1 February 2012

Dear World

It's February 2012 and already it's been a funny old year. I've been a single girl now for twelve months, during which time I have also started my own business, moved house, written a book, forgotten who I was, remembered who I was, and *that* was just the tip of the iceberg!

Such a lot has been happening in my Peachey life; yet that is no surprise – as a woman I'm a creature of many facets: I have a family, a past, a business, friends, hobbies, thoughts, feelings, talents and am made up of umpteen influences, inheritances, joys, sorrows and impulses.

So why am I writing these letters? Well, at the start of 2012 with the warm approach of February – the Valentine month of 'love', I decided to set myself a loving challenge – to write a love letter, every day of the month, to the crucial, critical and special people, phenomena and happenings in my life. At this point in their evolution I only have a vague notion of who, where or what I will direct my letters to... I know that God is going to get at least one letter, as are friends, family and other players in my life – be they alive, departed, or indeed, imagined...

My love letters are intended to entertain me, to allow me to be creative and be a writer; I want them to exorcise demons, to celebrate and give me the space to analyse, enjoy, and give thanks for my life. They are a loving challenge set to myself and to share with the world, shared so that I commit to completing them and facing my destiny... So, it's going to be an interesting twenty-nine days... who knows where it will start, end or go from here?

In this age of reality TV and soap-opera, so much is shared, so often. I'm not usually a fan of being a fictional or real fly on the wall – especially when I know there is a director and cameraman on hand. Often I find real life so much more fascinating, and of course, my *own* life to be the most fascinating one of all! So in the spirit of secrecy, you may not see *all* my letters here, as some may be *too* personal or share information that is the rightful possession of others, yet (at least) twenty-nine there will be, out there in the ether and my gifts to their receivers.

Well dear world, on that note, I'm tired and light headed and it's time to wind down to sleep now, so here endeth the first letter.

Lovingly yours

Sandra x

PS: Dear World – it's now August 2012 and I have reached my goal of twenty-nine letters... and now *more* come – unbidden and impelled; and thanks to the fabulous feedback of so many, have now transformed from blog into book. Wow dear World – thank you!

PPS: And as this letter was written on the 1st of February 2012, so all the other letters have followed and will now be undated, as they make their way into the world and follow their own Peachey logic...

That's me, walking towards my destiny.
Regents Park, London, July 2011

CHAPTER 1
The Seeds

Dad, me, Mum and Arthur, on a family holiday in
Cornwall, some time in the late 1960s

Letter to the Seeds

Dear Peachey Seeds

I remember the first time I saw the secret seeds of a peach… I was a teenager and preparing to devour an overripe juicy fruit. As I prised the flesh apart, the stone fell apart too and revealed, nestled therein, two almond-like seeds… Somehow I had always thought that the *stone* was the seed, but instead what was revealed to me was a seedy secret. It turns out that peaches will only yield their hidden treasure when ready – when trying to repeat the experience on the next peach, I managed to cut myself as the knife bounced off the stone and sliced instead into me, and that time red blood was added to peach flesh, and still those particular seeds stayed safe from sight.

So everything springs from some form of seed – whether known, or seen, or revealed, or indeed hidden in the ground to eventually transform into a tree. Yes, before the peach, first comes the tree and before the tree, is the seed…

And my dear Seeds, in the beginning and indeed before the beginning, are family, friends and companions. For all of us, they are those characters who have created us genetically, who have shaped us psychologically and have started and shared the pattern of ourselves and our own life journey – that very journey we are all on – sometimes in spite of, and sometimes because of, their influence on it.

From the various forms of counselling and coaching I've experienced, re-living and picking over our origins is so often the start of a process of reconciliation and healing: this can be if we are in crisis, or wishing to move on in or step up in our lives. These early life influences can conversely also be treated as unnecessary cargo – for not being important to the *now*, or considered a time-wasting indulgence in negative or unnecessary detail which distracts and distorts from the business of moving on. Being trained in various supportive methodologies has meant that variously I have been taught to either explore or ignore these primal ancestral maunderings; and so it is something I now deploy if the issue, emotion or situation suggests it... or not as the case may be.

In *this case* I will now give in to the well-rehearsed expectation that at the beginning of a coaching relationship, the coachee relives and remembers the history of the issue at hand – presenting it to the therapist to explore. And this of course has the value too of unburdening, of sharing, of analysing and seeing it all through a fresh pair of eyes. This act of sharing so often gives a degree of release in itself – therefore the fundamental act of sharing your earliest life, the events, influencers, family, friends, advocates and (so often) naysayers, has to be the ultimate starting point.

There is a lot contained in a seed – so many possibilities, so many paths to pursue and so it is, that this chapter introduction is longer and more detailed than the rest in the book, as the seed scene is set and expanded…

In writing my letters then, I find that I celebrate and contemplate those seeds who created me, influenced me and were around me in my beginning times.

One of my earliest seeds and hence once of my first written letters, provoked a huge emotional reaction and resonance from so many people…

The recipient – my father, was born and named Stanley Charles Peachey in the last year of the First World War. His home was in rural Cambridgeshire, where I spent many happy hours as child, on weekend visits to my grandmother, stumbling around the Fenland that her cottage was on the border of.

So to me and to him… My father was by trade a plasterer and after serving in India and Burma in the Second World War, he moved to Coventry to work in his builder brother's business – quite literally re-building a city shattered by German bombs. During the war he found Christianity and had come into contact with an ideological movement called 'Moral Re-Armament' (now known as Initiatives of Change). As a result he met and married another Peachey seed: my mother – Agnes Reynolds.

Early into the marriage my brother – Arthur was born, and another year or so later another baby boy – John, was stillborn. This loss added huge emotional stress to what was already in many ways a strained relationship, between two very different personalities, who together were not a conventional love match. To heal their difficult relationship, after years of tears and arguments, they decided to have another child.

They have both told me about my planned conception and since, by the time I was thought of, they slept in separate rooms, I can't imagine what that coming together was like for them. They spent two nights together in one room to make a baby. That's all it took. I was created. My dad became a father again at the age of 45.

He loved having a child in his middle age and always told me that I kept him young. Sometimes people assumed he was my grandfather, but these things don't matter to a child – well not to this one any way. And like any lifetime of memories – my memories of my father are not all perfect ones, but they are mostly happy ones. We adored each other and made each other laugh, and from beginning to end, would chat away endlessly about the serious and the sublime.

I always remember that I felt that he was never quite conventional… He didn't drink or smoke, so I grew up in a teetotal household. And it always seemed that he never did things the ways other dads did… The photograph in this book of the two of us and our co-created snowman demonstrates that perfectly… no ordinary snowman was ours – rolled and crafted and patted into shape… no – as a builder, he took a pragmatic view and filled his large stainless steel plasterer's bucket with snow and *moulded* one instead!

Eventually he reached retirement and I headed for university and then, older and possibly wiser, I returned home whilst I reached for the world of work and true adult independence.

Soon after that, my mother retired and so transitions and decisions had to be made. And instead of discussions or the usual arguments, it all just seemed to turn in on him and he started a descent to rapid insanity. My brother and I asked doctors to look at him, but they did nothing, so we tried to get social services to intervene. No one but us seemed to see that this was a desperate, dying man.

His death certificate records an unusual cause: 'Chronic duodenal ulcer, paralytic ileum'. Mind affected body or body affected mind – who knows?

Well, that was all a quarter of a century ago and despite the time lapse, still I felt impelled to write to him first of all, and thus came into being, the letter to my father.

So naturally now I move from my father, to the seed of my mother... As I started to write this book, my mother was 86, with a neurological condition called Parkinson's disease. She was wheelchair bound, having broken both her hips and having been in and out of hospital with physical and mental issues in the last few years of her life. At the time of writing the letter to her, she lived in a nursing home and needed assistance with all aspects of her life.

Half way through writing the book, she died... she was clearly fading, but still her passing was sudden and shocking to me. How can you really know what the passing of a seed will feel like, until it actually happens?

At the end psychologically it was mixed... she knew who her visitors were and what they were up to. She knew significant dates and liked to have a watch, clock and calendars so that she could track the days. Then again, in many respects, she was like a child, being toileted and dressed and throwing tantrums if she could not have her own way.

She was born in Dundee, Scotland, in 1926 – an only child, of what she regarded as a loveless marriage; hastily arranged because of her mother's pre-marital pregnancy.

This letter followed its own course and unbidden I found myself remembering too another seed – my mother's mother – my 'Nanna', of whom I remember so little, since she died when I was six years old.

My mother had found herself a 'victim' many times in life... of circumstance, of believed wrongdoing, of so many things. As a result, she has so often been unforgiving, and loud to protest, and has let many people in her life go... Whereas *I*, in contrast, so often cannot bear to let people loose from *my* life. As my maternal seed, I know that I am many things because of my mother and am also consciously NOT many things in deliberate contrast.

So often in my past, I have blamed my mother for my so-called life. A life without a marriage, without babies, without... so much that I craved for as a child. I blamed her for entrenching emotional attitudes in my psyche, for being loud and difficult, for creating her own hell on earth, for the negative effect she had on others I loved, for my cursed sensitivity as I trod delicately on eggshells, wondering if her mood was high or low, violent or loving...

And on my long journey to love and enlightenment, my mother has always been a huge mental phenomenon; and my own cursing, victimhood and blame were high, steep bridges for me to cross. And before she died I had crossed many of those archaic arches. I have realised lately, with love, that the life that she knew and the thoughts and reactions that ensued, were not of her doing, or of her choosing. She was somehow so often an outsider, and did not have the knowledge or support that I have sought and found, on my journey.

It comes as no surprise then, that my mother is one of my greatest lessons in life, an ongoing reminder and indicator of the burdens we feel we are born with and so often do not shed. And some of the things I have loathed about her – I not so secretly admired too... Her indomitability, her speaking out, her 'take me or leave me' attitude and that, in our story, love is both a birthright and a gift.

Despite everything, still she managed to astonish me with her love... The writing of this letter came about because of a surprise gift she arranged...

And so this is one story of my mother: maligned, redeemed and in the final analysis, cherished. And now she is gone, still so deeply and purely beloved by me.

Now I move along the family tree and so the *Letter to John* came to me, as I remembered and explored my feelings around a brother, who came before me. He was stillborn at six months and his passing was a crime and a deep pain in the life of my parents. So traumatic it was, that my living brother – at only two years old, can remember the day my mother went into premature, painful and very distressed labour.

John Peachey was born into and died in the 1950s, when there was no support network, no counselling, no real empathy or means of easing the emotional devastation that his loss must have wrought. It seems that instead there was simply an implicit expectation that my mother and father just had to get over it and get on with their lives.

And somehow, I connected the loss of my brother John with my grandfather – my mother's father, who also had died before I was born. He is a legend of my life, a colourful character, giving me so much of my inheritance. Born in Dundee, Scotland, he was a councillor and union man of strong left-wing and communist principles, which apparently led him to jail on more than one occasion. And this was not the only trouble that he got into – later having an affair, which resulted in a pregnancy. So he left his wife and adult daughter – to become a father again, this time to a boy. And not so long after that, he died, before his next child – a girl, was born.

Reflecting on this John never felt like loss, until that moment of reflection and then I remembered that there was *another* John, an uncle – lost to me too. This time there is loss since he is not knowingly connected to me. Yet here too I can *celebrate*, for of all the Johns, I truly trust that this one lives and that simple fact in itself then opens out so many questions. Who is he? How is he? What happened to him? I have in my possession photographs of him as a small child. Do he and his sister know they had an older sister? Do they have questions about their father that we can help to answer? I pray that one day, all these queries will be answered, yet for now – here is the letter to all my Johns.

And so from the seeds of family, to the sisterly seed of an early childhood friend who has been there, almost since the beginning. I am very blessed to have known my two oldest friends – Sue and Pinda, since I was five years old and now, nearly half a century later, we are still connected. That fact is such a joy to me. Where so many people have come and gone in my life, they chose to stay with me and I with them.

I am very blessed too in that I have a group of gorgeous people in my life I would call 'close' or best friends. Having these chosen people in my life has always been important to me. As it goes, we walk in and out of each other's lives – chattering, laughing and sometimes crying as we go. We share the soap-operas of each other's existences and stand back or have our say, and so we co-exist in many different spheres of our lives.

Do we consciously choose our friends or do they just happen to us? It is my belief that place and circumstance bring us together, then time will test us and see if we stay together.

The company we choose to keep is important. Do these friends mirror us, support us, love and cherish our being? Our friends can be part of our definition of ourselves, as they reflect and contradict qualities we treasure or deny. A true friend is a real treasure, a gift, an assistance, a joy, a physical and a psychological support.

So of all my friends, the letter wrote itself to Sue, possibly because we were closer, at an earlier age than all the others, and so have more interweaving histories from the beginning. I do feel there are letters out there, in the ether, waiting to written and read to so many others... Where do I start? Quite simply I have let the letters choose... now is that being creative or is it a cop out? I'll let you, the reader, decide ... And in my own indecisive defence, I will dub the letter to Sue, as one to my archetypal 'every friend', representing all our intermingling journeys, memories, dreams and of course, love.

These then are *my* seeds. See which seeds germinate for you during the reading of this chapter, see who springs to mind and into your heart – let them be sown unbidden and see too what grows out of them.

And so back to my dear Seeds – here ends your letter and here starts my first chapter.

Yours in loving awe

Sandra:
Grand-daughter, daughter,
niece, sister, friend and seed...

Peachey seeds
Mum and Dad on their wedding day

Letter to My Father

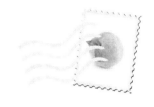

Dear Dad

How strange to be writing to you again. I can't have done that since 1984! And then you departed this life only two years later – after a traumatic three months, when I watched you slide down from life to death. It all seemed to be a horrible case of mind over matter. Did your mind or your body end you? It seems they both conspired. I can trace the day it started and then remember so clearly the day it all ended.

I tried to save you with love. I remember sitting with you in your bedroom and telling you that I loved you and you told me that while I sat there and held your hand, you felt sane. Yet that moment in time did not save you and still you left us that same Easter.

There I go... off at a tangent, starting at the end... still it's MY love letter and I know that you will love it anyway. One thing you never left me in any doubt about, was the fact that you loved me, that you were proud of me and that I was always wanted and appreciated.

I was a planned and wanted baby, born after a difficult period in a difficult marriage; the little girl that both parents hoped for. And you told me one day that you had a vision of me long before I was even thought of... the one female in your life that you would connect to like no other.

You told me too that I came out of the womb completely in charge and as soon as I could speak, I started ordering you around, which always made you laugh and so you were enraptured and amazed by my mature precociousness.

Thanks to you and the cosy nightly ritual of reading to me at bedtime, I have always loved books and the beauty of the written word, and even in the adult now, have a creative imagination that can quickly take me to the realms of dream and wonder.

Reflecting now Dad, I remember that you would sit in the kitchen of an evening, legs crossed; and as a tiny child I would sit in the crook of your foot and swing on your leg – riding my very own daddy swing, as I chattered away to you. I love the memories of us then, of being your daddy's girl. A gift to you in your middle age.

From you I get my sense of humour – we love puns and wordplays. You have a definite sentimental streak and would cry at a sad film. Then later in life you would drive me and my teenage friends around in one of your old cars, singing away at the top of your voice, completely unselfconscious; and I remember at the time thinking that it wasn't socially ideal, but it *was* funny and deciding that I would not be embarrassed. My friends would have to accept how it was, along with the ride – that it was all part of being with me and in my life.

And so we grew older, both of us. You always wanted me to be happy and never pushed me, though somehow at the end, when I came home to roost for a while, I became a little disenchanted with you. Maybe that just has to happen, that as children we have to move away psychologically, to live our own lives.

I always loved you though and what I am left with, a quarter of a century after you left this life, still, is that love. I have so many inheritances from you, both natured and nurtured and can sometimes see your handsome face in the mirror... and then it goes again and it's just my reflection, your unique angel, partly of your creation. And so here we are and now it's time for me, reluctantly, to end this letter.

I loved being in touch with you again Dad. Let's do it again...

Love you loads,

Sandie Annie xxx

Letter to My Mother

Dear Mum

Unexpected presents are fabulous aren't they? And I got one from you on Valentine's day. A bunch of peach-coloured roses and carnations... peach from a Mrs Peachey to a Miss Peachey... Thank you – so so much! For this I cried, with happiness, with surprise and appreciation, because this was such an act of generosity to me and not the easiest thing to organise when you are wheelchair bound, in a nursing home and not surprisingly, given everything about who and where you are now – in body, mind and environment, that it is usually all about *your* wants being met and met *now*! Is *that* where my natural impatience stems from, I wonder?

Several weeks ago I was hauled into the headmistress's – also known as the (nursing home) manager's office – to be told of bad behaviours, possible causes and then courses of action. I went to you next... 'Why did you do it?' I asked gently and you said there was a voice in your head telling you to... So that's what drives you on now... Which voice organised roses for me then, I wonder smilingly today? I must remember that, when the other, darker voice is at work on another day in our lives...

So this is our now. Mother becomes child. My brother and I take you out and about and have to look after every aspect of your care as we go. And one day I observed lightly that it was our karma

– we neither of us children had children, so now we were taking care of our version of child… My brother smiled back…

There is so much water under the bridges of our lives now. So many tears, so many shoutings, such anger, such blame. Yes blame, such a heavy, self-victimising blow of a word, of a deed. Oh I blame, blame, blamed you for so much, for everything, in between those times I thought I had struggled away to be a different creature, a creature of light and laughter, the blonde-haired cherub of your proud creation.

Then always I would return to you to break the news… that I was back in black… And more blows reigned on you – no grand-babies, no soft Nanna lisps to be loved and spoiled… my heart breaks to think you will probably never have that from your line.

From my babyhood on, I never doubted that you loved me, though at times you tried hard to disguise the fact, in some very extreme ways. Your own childhood was lonely, broken and unloving and you told me you had decided you would not repeat the histories of your mother and father's poor parental conduct, with your own children.

You were one child alone, a little girl with chestnut hair and an indomitable spirit, who refused to go to school one cold day because the colour of your tights weren't right… who skated, loved the cinema and had a cat called Spitfire… I loved those stories of your life back then. Though too there were the stories of betrayal, loss, ridicule and shame – the darker stories that were also woven into your life fabric.

And we shared more stories on long weekend afternoons when we watched old black and white movies on the sofa, together. You knew all the decades-old gossip of every star, gleaned from escapist movie magazines of way back when and I took it all in.

Then the tides of time turn and we grow up and grow old and there were more years and many more tears between us two.

It is an oddly natural thing to see a sort of reflection of you that is so similar and yet so very different. Sometimes your face appears in me, sometimes your voice and oft times I have called the dark chiding hateful voice sometimes spiralling in my soul – you too. 'You are just like your father' you would accuse, and he would sometimes say 'you're just like your mother' and then in another moment I would be different to her.

The constant family comparisons… The fascinating DNA lottery that gives us both blue eyes, me with blonde hair, you with dark. Father and brother with brown eyes, father dark haired, brother fair and so on and then our myriad talents, skills and personalities – our very mysteries of making, born and nurtured.

You were born in Scotland. I loved that – it marked me out, made me more exotic! Yet somehow

Scotland rubbed off, as you left it at 18 years of age; it did not hold in your voice and there were only small clues in our Sassenach lives… some words, some poems, a Broons annual… So a lot of your life was left behind there and I hardly knew any family from way back then, except for my Nanna – your own mother. You often compare me to her… my popularity, my nature, you said… that which is so different from one, is so like the other; now there is one particular photo of her cradling a baby me and looking at it now, you know exactly where I sprang from…

It is not for me to compare us in nature, since she left this world when I was six… just too young for remembering much except the gifts of sixpences and dark chocolate she would save for her grandchildren's visits to the dark little flat in Birmingham. But there is just one more happy story, amongst the many stories to be unfurled… You in hospital Mum, having just given birth to me and Nanna comes in to room so excited and cries 'where is she, where is she', wanting to meet and know me for the first time. And always that story was told with such pride and laughter.

And there is so much more, so many stories, so much to say and yet really, so little. Now it boils down to this – the blaming has had to STOP for me. I try to journey away from that, from so called past misdemeanours. It has taken so long and I kept on blaming until recent history, even when I had tried to fix, to analyse, to change.

Then one day I literally woke up and realised, that all those dark words and actions were not really you. Throughout all your life you have done the best with what knowledge and resources you have had; and so then I was just left to love. And love changed a lot, love created a force-field around me and radiated from me, to stop me barbing and griping... and without that, you had to love more too. Now it's not a complete cure... there are times when I am tired or facing a low moment and it surfaces again. Yet I know, come what may, that I have escaped hate and guilt and I can always say, truly, that I love you.

I love you, Mum.

Sandy Bach xxx

My Valentine gift from Mum...

Letter to John

Dear John

'Dear John' – that phrase in the world of cliché means the beginning of a 'goodbye'. Yet this time, for me, this is the beginning of a hello, a getting in touch, a getting to know you, to connect with you and so to deepen the connection with myself and to understand the role you have played in my life.

Do you know me John – your sister, the one that came after you? You had so little time in this living realm, a tiny baby, who did not see with living eyes the world you were born into.

Your passing was a pain, a grief, a darkness that reached into my time, born as I was five years after your passing. I always knew about you – and our mother told me that not one day went by when she did not think of you. And in tears and arguments, your memory would surface and be tossed around by our parents, a turmoil unresolved, unforgiven, never forgotten.

It's a dark place John, to think of the pain and the torment of your passing, so let me pass back to the realms of love and dreams and consequence…

We have a living brother of course, two years older still than you; and in my dreams I have seen you, another version of my family… familiar and yet separate.

So you were a fascination to me, part of my puzzle, a missing strand of DNA. And as a child I often imagined how you would be, if you walked in this world.

And I have realised over time that had you stayed in this world, then I probably would not be here, as I am, in this form, in this living plane of being. So I thank you John and it's a complicated thank you, for your part in who I am. And because of your passing and my safe and happy arrival; my parents were so overjoyed to welcome me when my time came to enter this world. And separately they have both told me that I was their saviour, angel child, which feels like a beautiful privilege sometimes and at other darker times, an expectation that I have felt I simply could not live up to.

You were named John for our grandfather – our mother's father. Another John gone before I was born, another John not known by me. Though for *this* John I have photographs, stories and a history... This John stands in line in our parent's wedding photos and his physical features sometimes reveal themselves in the living descendants that are my familiars. This John is part of our Scottish heritage and so Grandpa John was also known as 'Jock'. And I can only guess at what other inheritances we have all got from him. I would love to explore that part of my past puzzle one day if I can...

And one of the many legends of Grandpa John is that he has another family, one that came after my mother; the fact of which was scandal at the time. So my mother would say that she is an only child and so she was in fact until her mid 20s. In recent years she has sought to know her later siblings – a half brother and sister and so I have traced the pieces of paper that would link us to them.

But what comes next? Do they know of us? Do they know they have a sister, niece and nephew? And here's the thing too, my (half) uncle out there, somewhere, is also John, named for Grandpa John too – and takes his first name *and* his surname.

Another John not known to me, now old enough to be retired… is he still alive, does he have his own family, what did he do with his life? Could he be a piece of the puzzle that fits, or could he care less? I stopped the search because my mother, his half sister, became ill and needed our attention and now, further down that line, for many reasons, I'm not sure whether to pick it up again.

Whatever the case, I am trusting that this John lives and loves and laughs. And of my three Johns – brother, grandfather and uncle, it is Uncle John who comes into my mind most of all, now I'm at this time in my life. My father gave us an uncle and two aunts who have all left this world now, so it's good to know that there is more family out there and maybe, at the end of this letter, that's all I need to know about them.

We all have our legacies, our legends and live with the consequences of love – our own loves and the love that was created by those who went before us.

In the final analysis I want to connect to the love; live and breathe it in every form and on that note I will bid all my Johns, for now, a very fond farewell.

With love from Sandra xxx

PS. Thanks go to my brother and mother who agreed to let this letter be seen and for reminding me that when I was in my pram, we used to visit my brother John's tiny grave. A connection unremembered… and one for which I am grateful. *S x*

Grandpa John, a face known and unknown...

Letter to Sue

Dear Suzy Blue

I'm wondering how to start this letter, as we've known each other such a long time, haven't we – since we were five in fact. And I'm blessed with two best friends I've known since then, how fortunate am I? So that's a lot of history, yes many many photos, stories, smiles and sobs. All part of love and of life.

So Suzy Blue, the story of me and you started at infant school. There were shared lessons, scandals and whispers. You were always the model student, with good grades and neat handwriting. I would get told off for talking in class, sometimes praised for my brilliance, sometimes chided for my lazy ways. At the end of the school day we would walk home, down the streets of our childhood, where we would reach your house first, say goodbye and then I would troop the last few streets alone back to my home and hearth.

We were two in a group of four girls, who together shared endless childish summers, making mud pies in summer gardens; then hopping on the bus to dance classes or swimming, all mixed in with endless chatter, laughing and boasting. The other two girls are lost through time, occasionally glimpsed, part of the fabric of our lives.

My quiet weekends were boldened and brightened by the trips out to the countryside, the pair of us in the back of your dad's car. On the best trips of all, there was a corned beef sandwich wrapped in wax paper, or the ultimate treat... a glass of lemonade in a pub garden on a summer's day.

The next phase in our lives meant we went to the same senior school, but amongst the 1500 girls there, we found ourselves at different ends of the campus, catching glimpses of each other and now just dipping in and out of each other's lives. We had newer friends and walked different paths.

The clock turns again and we found ourselves together in the comfy chairs of the sixth form common room. We rediscovered our friendship and created our kinship. Then we embarked on Bacardi and coke, school discos and boys...

The adult world beckoned and changed the ties, my Suzy Blue. You went out into the world of work, whilst I finished my A levels. Then off I went to university and you became a nurse. Still we kept in touch and that far off time, was probably the last time I wrote you a letter. Hundreds of miles away at my northern university home, letters were such a lifeline and each one was devoured and re-read and savoured, as they chronicled our ascent into adulthood.

After gaining a certificate, cap and gown, I returned home and we picked up where we left off, becoming closer still; pretty much living in each other's pockets and still having alternative lives with family, friends and men. I practically lived at the hospital digs in your tiny bedsitter room. One of my favourite memories of then, is you and me walking home from the night club at two in the morning –

an endless three miles home, taxi not an option... in our bare feet, our high heels dangling from our hands... ah – burning feet, happy days!

And as they loaded us into a car, with our holiday suitcases, our mothers said how they could not imagine the other one not being there... like sisters they said...

Then men happened... then a baby – your first baby, my goddaughter Elizabeth; so the edges of our relationship shimmied and altered. Then work, more babies, the process of growing up and going through life.

You, now a married women with three children, nourishing and nurturing the next generation. An amazing mother, putting in so much love, so much effort and so much time. The boundaries of our relationship altered again and still we became closer. I became part of the family. Me now cool 'Auntie' to Elizabeth, Jenny and James. There were holidays in caravans, soothing baby tears, watching the children grow and along the way a myriad of shared sorrows and joys. Part and not part of your family, part of the in-crowd of grandparents, in-laws, brothers, sisters, nieces and nephews...

And when my father died, you were there and when your father died much later, I was there and that is how it was.

And time ebbs and it flows and then it took you away from me to live in Africa. So I grieved for a while and when we phoned each other, we would nearly always be in tears, letting the other know they were missed and loved. You came back to me though, you always do.

And then a shock – you became a grandmother! Yes, that makes me a great aunt! Look: you know your friends will bring children into your life, but now time and love take on a whole other amazing dimension...

Well Suzy Blue, that is me and that is you. And there are times when you are gone from me again and yet I don't grieve now, because after so many years, we are wiser and warmer. And we know that wherever we are, we love each other, through sharing and friendship and time; and every now and again, we remind each other of that gorgeous big little fact – don't we?

Lots of love n stuff,

Sandra xxx

You and me on your wedding day ...

CHAPTER 2

The Stone

A quiet, contemplative me, on holiday in Turkey

Letter to the Stone

Dear Stone

I am writing to you, even though you are usually
ignored and discarded, extraneous as you are to the
serious business of eating and drinking. Your hard,
horny exterior excludes and repels. Yet dear Stone,
you have a very real purpose and you are diligent
and excellent at the performance of your role. Well
that is, if excellence is rated on a scale for Peachey
protection. Your rough and pitted exterior is like the
Rolls Royce of safes – guarding its seeded treasure
within: so dutifully, so silently, so relentlessly. It is
practically impossible for the average mortal to pry
you open, unless you are primed and ready to reveal
what is within.

You protect and you keep the seeds safe, yet so often
the seeds are not revealed and so do not see the light
of day. Never shall those protected seeds respond
to water and the warmth of soil, and hence will not
fulfil their destiny... Whole orchards lie in discarded
peach pits – bearing no blossom, leaves or fruit, nor
shade, nor future seed...

So the stone will keep its seeds safe, but it shall also
keep them small. They cannot grow against the
confines of their curving walls; instead they are kept
firm and small in their imprisoned place. The stone
is stronger than the seed, as it binds and confines.

Then the stone reveals that it has many more facets
and one of the secrets that it keeps is the *Letter to*

My Clown. Clown and stone: twinning sounds, each five letters long. The clown seems to be out there posing and dancing in the sun, yet clowns too are so often about anarchy and darkness and have a painted on cover, just as the stone has its hard pitted purple exterior. And so too do clowns exist in the circus ring, just as the seeds stay right and tight, tucked inside the circle of the stone's shell.

Yet sometimes the stone is ready to reveal: it softens, it cracks open and yields up its soft sweet treasure of seeds. The stone disintegrates and reveals the softness therein, just as I reveal and revel in my softer *Letter to Daftness*. The clown transmutes from dark to daft and eventually, I lovingly leave the stone behind, to open up myself the light and to the rain.

And still, so often, I re-encounter my old enemy – resistance: that black blinding and binding force that prevents me from wandering over the seen and unseen boundaries of my existence. Will you never be far from me? It is as if I am encased again and again in a dark, pitted peach stone of a prison. So it seems that I cover myself in a horny shell, not doing or being anything other than fearful or neutral. And then I realise that even knowing what you are, means that the shell starts to thin and then I can see the light and so I can move stumbling or dancing, towards the light and crack the shell wide open.

And somehow I dared to write a *Letter to God...* The God who has kept me small and confined, just like the shell – well, that is what I have *blamed* him/her for... I realise too that the *Letter to God* belongs in this chapter, since God-ness, spirituality, our higher self, the other dimension – however you might label it – not only surrounds us, but is at the very core of everything we do; just like the stone – with its soft centre and hardened cover, sitting snugly at the centre of every peach.

So I can see your sense dear Stone. Safety is important, it is primordial, it is psychological; and yet for the peach tree to grow, the stone has to crack and dissolve, in order to let in water and light.

And instead of the seeds nestling in their dark womb – they should know that the sky is out there, that they have to push against their walls; that they have to grow, to change, and to transform in order to become trees. Trees are not ideas, desires or dreams – trees are a solid force of nature, out there, weathering the elements and constantly growing. And by the act of growing, they then beget and bear fruit.

Every single peach tree was once a seed; a seed that broke free of the stone. So dear Reader, what is *your* stone, your protection, your reasons for staying small and safe? Know them and name them and then you can learn to plant the seeds, out side their protective stone.

In all your hardened glory, I thank you dear Stone for keeping me safe; and I *love* you dear Stone for breaking open and setting me free.

Yours freely and softly

Sandra Peachey

Letter to My Clown

Dear Martrucio

You may wonder why I'm writing to you when I haven't even been aware of you for very long – well not dressed in your circus suit any way. Yet you always seem to have been with me and now I know your name, it all seems to make sense...

So now we've been formally introduced, I have decided to write you a love letter and make sense of you, because otherwise I'm likely to blame you for a lot of things, or else curse you for being part of my life.

You were introduced to me a couple of weeks ago by a very wise Celt called Gill. One of her gifts is to help people identify and work with their 'archetypes'... these for me being facets of my self and hence my destiny. Getting to know my archetypes has provided me with some new revelations about my life, character and actions – and I thought I *already* knew me! As it happens, I *did* know me and now I know me differently, and I can never know enough.

But I digress – this is *your* letter Martrucio, so let's get back to you... Gill told me about my clown and I knew somehow that your name was Martrucio. Yes, you've always been around in some way, shape or form; and way back when – the first name I gave to you, was 'accident-prone'. For 'name' you can substitute 'label', a reason, an excuse, a hook to hang happenings on. You've gone by many names and at other times, people have called you ditzy, klutz, blonde or stupid. And because of you, I have been shouted at, cursed and you have been the cause of much embarrassment, apologies and use of cleaning fluids...

Why oh why Martrucio, even yesterday, when I had been getting acquainted with you, did you sit me next to the speaker at the event, the very event where I wanted to impress people, to sell them my services, be entertaining and respected and – well, all sorts of things really. So Martrucio, when the speaker tried in vain to get everyone's attention by tapping on a coffee cup with a spoon, did you prompt me to bash the wine glass full of orange squash with a heavy knife? Why Martrucio, why? Well it *did* get everyone's attention and maybe the sight of orange squash gushing out of the glass, onto the speaker's paperwork, her cream coloured jacket and the crisp white table cloth was entertaining, but really Martrucio, it was not quite the effect I wanted! I wanted to feel elated, but instead felt mortified – what on earth?!

So in that moment, the clown had a sad face. Yet fortunately the speaker survived and we're laughing about it now, so you are smiling again Martrucio – that big, red, grotesque, exaggerated mouth of a smile.

As time has gone on, I forget so often that you are in my life and then you re-surface – sometimes in mild form, sometimes extreme – so I crack a joke, which goes down well, then I crack a plate or bash my car – drat and curses! In some sense do I need you in my life Martrucio – I like to perform, to entertain, to detract, to bewitch; but then I would rather that what actually manifests is more glossy and impressive than the breaking and mucking up of things.

I was so relieved when years ago I saw a doctor who told me your name was 'inner ear balance problem' – at last I was vindicated, I had a *reason* to do all this stuff – something beyond my control – hurrah – a 'condition'! Other people have called you 'dyspraxia' – apparently all the signs are there...

There is a sense too, that often people see *you* Martrucio and not *me*, as I want to be seen. But it's time to let all that go.

You see now I know what your name is and that you are part of my being, my very infrastructure. I now wish to make my peace with you Martrucio and live with you in harmony – instead of the very up and down thing we've had going together for such a long time. The accidents are just a small part of what we do together. And get this Martrucio, I would now love to take our relationship to the next stage, though I'm not sure yet what that stage is. Let's just agree, lovingly, that I will allow you your time in the spotlight, and in return can you love me back and change where the spotlight shines please?

Thank you so much for listening Martrucio and I really want to thank you for making me smile and for showing me that it's OK not to be perfect and for giving me the gift of laughter and yes, maybe the ability to occasionally squirt people in the eye with a well aimed jet of flowery water...

With love, from Sandra x

Letter to God

Dear God

Today I am saying dear 'God' and that's what you have been for much of my life, although sometimes, rarely, I have denied you altogether, since you didn't seem to make any sense. Then again there was a long period where I lazily hedged my bets and said that you MAY exist, for how could I know for sure?

I learned of you via religious/Christian family ties, at church, at school and through my bedtime childish prayers.

I have spent much time with you, neglected you often too and now, we seem to co-exist, I believe, happily, most of the time.

But we know you and I, that there are times when I have fallen out with you, because I just believed, that you had got it wrong, that you were causing and inflicting unnecessary pain and suffering. That you were, basically, to blame. For if *you* had created *me*, then how could I be the cause of all this so called misery, in the way that many modern wisdoms would dictate?

And there have been times, even very recently when I *really* wondered what in heaven you were playing at... why you had created this turn of events, this misfortune of constant occurrences. I just wouldn't let you off the hook... I cried, I begged, I ranted and I cursed and still you stayed your course. Falling out with you is such hard work and I hate being angry, but I was so angry with you. Yes, I can say it, I was so very angry with God. Where could I go with that? What higher authority could I appeal to?

I just had to find the way, get it out of my system, in every way – body, mind and soul... so you waited patiently... rock of ages. Even when I blamed you angrily for all sorts of things – minor imperfections of happenings, broken things, difficulties, trips and tears.

At times like these you are GOD. Masculine, patriarchal, bound in church stone. In this God guise, I have accused you of being fusty, cruel and callous.

Yet as I have moved away from church, I have stayed with spirit and so you have transferred and transformed to Gaia, to Mother Universe; you are the spirit behind and beyond the physical world. The universe is life force, creation, vibrancy, love and fortune. The universe is flow, positivity, she guides and glows and takes you with the flow.

The universe is friend, is on my side, giver, sunshine provider... mother of all.

So as you have facets, then my love will flux and alter with the tides of your being, in both my mind and my heart. Love shapes and forms and one expression of love is prayer. I pray in many ways now, putting my intentions out there, expressing my gratitude, sharing the love. This very letter is a piece of prayer.

I make my peace with you now, well most of the time; though it seems I ride a roller-coaster so often and I'm not sure what will ever change that. I used to ask for an even keel… that wasn't to be. Instead I play out the soap-opera of my being, entertaining those around me with my constant stellar happenings, my seeming unconventionality, my breakages, my laughter… well maybe that is my purpose, my created path or maybe just a part of my own eternal puzzle of being. So I surrender…

You are always the ultimate constant; so please forgive me, please teach me, please help me to see the way and shine the light – yes shine a light for me so that I can shine a light for others… for that is when I experience real love. And the love of God that passeth all understanding is a gift, and a gift I greedily and gladly receive.

Thank you, for everything.

Love, Sandra

Letter to Resistance

Dear Resistance

'Love your enemy' is the first phrase that comes into my head right now. The reason being that I sat down and pondered who or what to write to next; as I am now so tantalisingly near to finishing my cherished challenge of writing a love letter a day, every single day, for the Valentine month of February. That is twenty-nine epistles… shooting out into the cosmos, reaching into the void… maybe to overreach and be sent unseen; or maybe to touch and to torch another creature's flame. Well so it should be, if indeed twenty-nine there were in existence. For I stared at a white page and racked a blank brain for an object of inspiration… and there was none… Just five letters to go… the end in sight, but now no sight, no sense of next.

So then suddenly, there it was – my enemy: resistance, procrastination, faffing, dawdling, dreaming, distracting or whatever name you are going by today… Now I want to have this out with you and I'm guessing this won't be once and for all: this stalling, this staying, this stopping of my strived-for success.

Why can't I move beyond this solid wall, this barrier, this self-created strange protectionism? Why am I so static, so staid, so very stuck, so often? What weight is this, what darkness, what blindness to my future? What rocket, what change or what challenge will shift you out of my path and let me stride, rather than stress my self forward? I am so staggered that not even grief, tears or terrible fear motivates me on and over you.

So I must consider this and think... well... could it be that now is not my time to move; or maybe here is my lesson – my learning obstacle to be climbed up and over and scaled like any average mountain of life. But then this mountain is unseen, and it feels so solid, so heavy, so truculent, so frustrating, so scream generating; if I let it stick and let it raise steam... There I am pulled back to black – stale, pale and aged.

So forward now... I see you and I raise you... I am aware of you and I name you. Not to shame you, though shame is tempting, but to acknowledge you, to understand you, to know your role, to push your boundaries, then to blast through to freedom.

Someone told me there is no real cure. 'My name is Sandra and I am a procrastinator'... I wait for the acknowledged applause to die away...

Now I name you and know you Resistance, I can start to step away from you, to walk around, climb over or sail in you. I know how you tick, I see how you move, I hear your special solid voice. That voice is not to be a vice to me now. For in the very act of stopping me, I learn to step around you, to dance nimbly away.

For me the solution is to share. Your weight is too much to bear alone. Life is not meant to be one. I choose to connect to cherished colleagues, not fellow workers, not sharing inmates. I choose to commit to promises, rather than to (other's) deadlines; I move to the light, to the way forward, in ways that work for me – that work with my rhythms, my wants, my true skills, my loves. I trace the naturalness of my form, my thoughts, of my heart and I replicate that out into the world. Then I choose to share the un-natural, the unwanted tasks and transferences with those who have the gifts that are my strangers, my sloth and my burdens.

This is not one lesson learned and kept close. So very often I slip back, absorbed into alternate realities, distracted by your square solid form blocking out the sun. I forget you are there, lulled into old life patterns, long learned forms of being and of seeing. Now in my new life there is no pattern of average days to give me reason and meaning, so I choose to create my own way and my freedom. And freedom is not resistance, it is grace and flow and ease... and *these* I love. So smugly I will end – my very enemy now my friend, and now my very latest letter.

Farewell old friend.

Not yours. Miss S E A Peachey

Letter to Daftness

Dear Daftness

That alliteration is a great start to a letter... It is easing me in gently, with a smile, as I start to contemplate you... dear Daftness...

Close family and friends know I have a certain delightfully, or dangerously daft quality; and to the world at large I often try to cap it or limit how much I show of it... It's there though, part of who I am and what I do...

The thing with me is, that I love to present a professional and polished gloss to the world... Yet, so often, I'm daft... And that's not a criticism of myself – it's a simple description... And growing older and wiser (as well as dafter...) I've learned more and more that it's OK to show these true colours, and embrace them, and let the world see them; and then the world can decide to shirk me for it, love me for it or indeed not give a damn about my daftness... so there it is, in all its daft technicolour glory...

So Daftness is... being forgetful, being late, being trivial, being accident-prone, being indecisive, being wantonly childish, losing self-control. Sometimes it is so much me that it feels like my own brand of alien significance – defining me, slowing me down, making me cry with frustration or laugh with the Peachey familiarity of it... Daftness...

And I wonder what the reader will think – those that know me in body and place… Is that the me they recognise? And for some it may be a shock that I believe this of myself, and others will smile in recognition… and for others again, it may just open more doors onto their own knowing of me… and for others still, who know me from these letters alone – mere anecdote…

Now, I have consciously drawn into my orbit those that I can safely be daft with… Because sometimes, believe you me, I have been vilified for it and lost jobs and people in my life because of it… Yet it is *me*… imprinted in my DNA, I simply can't change it… Though if I try hard… I can manage it and have done a damn good job of presenting my 'got together' professional face to the world; but that can be hard work sometimes… and more often than not – my inner clown will trip me up or show me up, and the spotlight shakes the real me out into the open.

So, true to Peachey form, at times I am good with the daft, and at times I truly hate it. And though I *knew* that being daft and proud is all good, I probably never really *got* that, until these last few weeks since my mother's passing… She died two weeks ago and so at times my brain is the consistency of a marshmallow, and I can feel like a little lost orphan, and 'doing' or deciding what to do with a day is difficult; and 'being', and being in certain places is really hard work; and patience is thin and energy is low, and the daftness quotient goes through the rude roof.

At times too, I'm on top of the world and out there in it – being amazing... it is indeed weird to be me right now... My mother passing has somehow brought out some of the worst in me and all of the best me of me, and made me 'more so' – in just about *every* way.

So love is a complicated and many splintered thing, and this is, of course, a love letter to Daftness. I'm definitely more daft right now... but you know what? I've realised that it is all good; I've decided to give in to it and to embrace it. I know that being daft is perfect for me right now and I'm going with the daft flow. I'm being vulnerable, I'm being selfish, I'm being real. I give permission to the daft and I welcome it. It's like a soft blanket of sweet childishness. Being daft right now means I have a freedom when it comes to taking care of myself, or telling others what I want, and to do as much or as little of what I feel capable of doing and giving right now...

And in this state of being, work has not been a priority, but then the world turns in such a way that without even trying, I am suddenly given new opportunities and new clients... And even in these strange and newly motherless times – when I speak and when I coach, I forego 'daft' and create magic instead...

So being soft and being daft has allowed friends and strangers to care for me and support me even more than they have before. And from surrendering in this way, I've gained so much. I've grown so much. And who knows, I may just stay openly daft, to everyone, forever... Or the hard shell, with the cracks in it, may return... Yet somehow I predict that there will be more raw, deft daftness; more freedom and more expansion of my soul... Yes – after the daftness comes the light and so it is that I have moved from one four-lettered word – d a f t to another – l o v e.

Now both daftness and love define me – and so it is that I have written yet another Peachey letter to love.

Yours beguilingly, blondely and daftly

S xx

CHAPTER 3
The Flesh

Snow walking in February 2012

Letter to the Flesh

Dear Peachey Flesh

It seems so often dear Flesh that you are the purpose of the peach... the flavour, the substance and the point of a peach. You are the very product of the peach, the reason for cultivation and consumption.

Yet far from being predictable – you are mutable: the colour of your differing forms, vary from hues of ripe white, through to a creamy tangerine tint and then the exaggerated orange of the canned, syrupy version of your fleshy self.

To me, dear Flesh you are the reward: the marvel of the melba, the jewel hidden in a tall, cool sundae, and so too are you the magnificent nectar produced from the woody ordinary-ness of an orchard tree. Your fleshy fibres give way to fruit, to juice, an aroma and an exotic eroticism of gorgeous taste.

The flesh of the peach: cut or pulped to serve a delicious purpose, to flavour and to fill, and to add fruity colour and candour to our eating experience.

Without the flesh of the peach we would survive. Yet without it, there is less; life is more neutral; our choices narrow to apple and orange – the ordinary fruit salad options that bring a blander sweetness to our lives.

For sometimes there is an abundance of peach and sometimes it is seasonal. And a peach can be everyday ordinary or exotically extraordinary, depending on your level of appreciation or the scale of its availability.

To celebrate life is to know the flesh – those secret and not so secretive pleasures and indulgences that make life more bearable and worth living. Far from being guilty pleasures, they expand the whole experience of life, so let's always feel free to explore the flesh, to feel its finesse and to love the fact that is part of who we are...

Devouring the flesh of the peach can be a savoured indulgence or a simple fact of stock. So too are my fleshy rewards in life, the Peachey phenomena and chosen gifts that can be ignored or appreciated. I choose to appreciate, to analyse, to understand and give gratitude for the 'Peachey Flesh' in my life and so, to my *Letter to Snow*.

Snow... an act of God or a gift from God, sometimes beautiful and sometimes barbarous. Snow is a force of nature: sometimes forced on my world; somehow both enhancing and endangering it. Yet if I see its beauty and its glory (rather than its danger) – then it truly is a delicious reward, just like the flesh of the peach. And food to me too is a reward, which is why it merits its very own letter. Food for me is Peachey pleasure, tasting treasure, quite simply symphonic delight for the tongue. Love in a bowl, on a plate, in my mouth, then into my tummy. A book of Love Letters to my Peachey life would simply be incomplete without it.

Then there is the *Letter to Photographs* – an invocation to my own heavenly hoard of creation and memory. Pictorial peaches every one, fruit-like fleshy reward in multiplicity, stored on cardboard and in digitality.

And so from cardboard reward to my *Letter to Song*. The sounds that fill me up and breathe out of me; and which can cause me to dance and to celebrate. The sounds that shall add to sadness one day and then raise you to glory and set you free on another, sunnier day, for the ghost of a moment or the length of an opera. We don't need song to breathe, to be alive; but we must breathe in order to sing and so song is one of the ultimate fruity, fleshy and hence Peachey rewards of life.

So there you go dear Peachey Flesh: that is you, in a love letter, brought together, enhanced and enjoined and so now, on, to your sister letters...

Yours Peachey-ly

Sandra

Letter to Snow

Dear Snow

Saying 'dear Snow' feels sort of unnatural, but then why should it? Snow is one of the most natural things in this corner of the world; a force of nature... a simple weather feature... mere frozen water transformed into magic or... a sheer pain in the arse?

So, how do I love snow? Well, there is what snow brings – a gorgeous luminescent sky, the magic of white cold flakes falling from heaven – filling the horizon with the promise and excitement of transformation.

For snow *is* transformative: the landscape is altered, filtered and changed in so many dimensions. There is the sight – a cool, white blanket covering the horizon; purifying, electrifying, cleansing and sculpting the landscape to wind-blown topiary peaks or a smooth unifying pure concrete.

And look closely into snow and you discover that it is woven from crystalline magic, being formed of diamonds and stars into a myriad of patterning that gives you a tiny glimpse of God.

Then there is the sound: an electric silence, feet crunching and compacting the pureness to footprint, shrieking happy children pelting snowballs and creating future be-wintered memories of sledging and snowmen.

And people tell me that they can smell snow coming. I don't sense snow that way, its appeal for me is the lack of that sense... another cleansing apparition, another altered state of being. A deprivation to add to the sensation.

The feel is multiple – the shiver of the anticipated shock of freezing cold; the sudden solidity transformed by warmth to water. Snow can be the solid force that is shaped into missiles and carrot be-nosed, old scarf dressed snow people – that jocular cousin to the scarecrow. It can be sticky and clingy, grabbing onto the fibres of your protective clothes. And snow can be white dust skimming the wintery land – powdery and ephemeral and formless.

As it fades, it melts and disappears, changing from its pure white form to the halfway house of sludge – snow now blackened, dimmed and dirtied by the environment underneath and around – reasserting itself and infecting the cool whiteness with a creeping blackness. And then there is snow melted and re-frozen... that smooth form of treacherous ice that brings bruises, breaks bones and slows us to protective caution.

The emotion is child-like and primordial. There is a heightened sense of homeliness, of being safe inside, peering out of the window; knowing there is a warm security, a cosy certainty enhanced by comfort food, extra warmth and other winter indulgences.

So Snow, this is your love letter and love is many splendoured thing. Yet it can be a complicated, contradictory thing too. For the light, white stuff has a dark side too and I tried not to think of this before I headed out into your path last night.

I hedged my bets… I would be safe because you were starting to fall and had not yet formed yourself into solid danger; it was a Sunday, so you would not have caused too much crazy world-stopping chaos and I decided I would respect your power and be careful, mindful and remember all the snow wisdom I have ever been taught.

Combined with darkness, your power turns darker; add in side-winding wind and you become an even fiercer force to be reckoned with. Even on the motorway where the cavalier speed merchants usually ride my bumper or flash by me in the fast lane, everyone respected you and slowed to snow pace. I so wanted to be home and warm and out of your way, yet joined the convoy of caution until the time came to branch off to my local little motorway.

I was all alone in the dark until I reached thickening slush and the next convoy of caution – feeling its way down towards Coventry at thirty miles per hour. I kept my calm and joined the crawl and still the adrenaline quickened in my blood, to flash out when I braked and my brakes fought and ignored me and then slowly acquiesced and slowed my car down – unlike my heart, which was beating faster and faster. I kept my nerve and whispered loving comfort to myself to see me through the ever-shortening distance home.

Then turning the corner to my final descent, the car slid and skidded – just for a second and then was in my control again, facing forward, heading home, cautiously maintaining momentum as I drove through your thickening layers along country lanes, where I had to guess the lines of the road from the hedge rows and my local land lore.

More careful twists and turns and finally came my home strait, my street, my relief.

So snow, your power is mutable, variable, a kiss on the landscape, a potential kiss of death. And that too adds to your thrill. Friend and foe snow. Love and loathe snow.

Snow – you are an infinite force to be reckoned with and isn't that, after all is said and done, so very like love itself?

With much love, regards and respect.

Sandra

Letter to Food

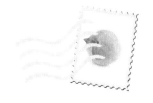

Dearest Food

If music be the food of love play on… if music be the love of food, game on… if food be the driving force of all else, then I'm a very happy girl…

Food drives our physical life; it fuels this temporal body and is one of the longest, most enduring loves of my life…

You see it all starting with a tiny baby, curling its toes with pleasure at milk time and then moving on to the natural strangeness of solids.

It is a fundamental love and though *you* may eat to live, I most definitely live to eat and I *love* to eat. So call me a gourmet, call me a foodie or call me a greedy hog… that is how it goes with me.

There is the pleasure of preparation… first the shopping – the choosing, the selection, the lingering dreamings of meals to come. Then gathering everything together for the feast: assembling, fettling, chopping and stirring the raw elements into a new, delicious entity. Testing, tasting, tempting yourself with what is to come.

The impatience of waiting and finally… readiness, yummy-ness and happiness, as you consume your labour of love.

Taste... an oft-neglected sense. Often ignored, when it should be pampered, praised and perfected for the pleasure and glory of sustenance.

So I devour my love in every way. I treasure and hoard cook books, slavering and anticipating over pages of pictures and food words.

For years I have pursued ingredients... herbs, flavourings and spices of every hue. My freezer is filled with future joy. I love the unusual, the divine, the out of the ordinary. Then, when rooting through the hoarding places, there are numbers that read 'out of date' – by years and years and so, I harden my heart and toss them out, unconsumed, unloved and left to moulder in the outside world.

Eating is an entertaining, an ecstasy. It takes you on voyages of new adventures, outside your door... in its pursuit I haunt and hunger around restaurants, cafes and tea shops, regard the menus – the very lists of love – and then wait for the love to arrive and so to begin.

Cooking for someone is an act of love... you are nourishing, treating and testing them. And for 'cook' read 'make a slice of toast' or 'create an elegant five-course dinner party'. The whole range of complexity is included here – it is *all* love. Though the toast *must* be made from the best bread, taken close to burning point, then spread to every corner with melting butter; part soft, part crisp, all delicious...

Food is reason enough to share, to come together. A social mixture, a treasuring of family and friends.

The way to a man's heart is through his stomach... yes food is proof of love, to man or woman or child. Food celebrates and food cements the tidemarks of all our lives.

Food forms the structure of our days, punctuating our playings and our labours.

Food takes you on journeys, food tells the stories of a place, of its history and flavours and impacts.

Food is always there for you, greedily needed, a constant craving.

So whatever way you look at it... food is love.

Forever yours

Sandra...

The end of a great meal, in Morocco...

Letter to Photographs

Dear Photos

Well I don't know about love... really it's more of an obsession...

I love those moments captured in time, I love memories revived, I love staging and posing and yet again the naturalness of a split millisecond of beauty or freeze-framed action.

I hoard, I treasure, I capture on camera. I love photography as an artform, as part subject/part picture-taker's product. I love that they can provoke an emotional response in me and I will devour their pixels again and again. And photography can be instant – a quick snap taken on your phone or it can be orchestrated, seen through a long lens, filtered by light, changed by perspective and by these means it can be glamorised or turned to black and white. It is life seen through an artificial eye... life that can be cropped, coloured and manipulated by machine to another identity, an altered ego, a new id changing our form through light and digitality.

And in this instant age, we can flash our images immediately around the world and sit back and wait to be 'liked' for it...

Of course I can loathe too – that wrong moment, that piece of flesh seen and frozen for public view. Yet I can quietly forget those images, un-name myself, just delete that piece of camera memory; and so photography becomes a polished performance of simply the best of me, of my times, my loves and my creations.

In my hoarding places, literally thousands of photos live, sometimes in the dark, sometimes to breathe lighter air... I have sepia representations of great-grandparents, babies now grown up and old, records of places travelled to and of loves lost and friends found...on cardboard and in computer they wait... to be seen and to be loved...

So look around my book and see a fraction of all the pictorial love I possess... a life of love in photographs...

Mind the birdie...

Sandra x

One of my all time favourite photos - of me with
my two oldest friends – Sue and Pinda

Letter to Song

Dear Song

I am puzzling over whether to address you as song singular or songs plural... either way, you know what I mean and you know how much I love you. In fact I love you so much that I am semi convinced that the reason my memory is so slow, is that my brain is simply overloaded with song lyrics... especially ones from the 80s... oh and the ABBA back catalogue of course...

I love listening to you, I love singing you, and I *really* love dancing to you. There I was this very evening in fact – dancing the night away and singing along; part of a jostling happy crowd, in the semi darkness of a singing, dancing, drinking, homage-ing kind of a place and, it has to be said, doing justice to all three of those activities... ah, the power of the multi-tasking woman...

And from childhood I saw myself as pop star, opera star, musical star... yes I would open my tonsils, so the dream went, and out would come a voice of such power and beauty that glass would shatter and icebergs would melt... When I sat and watched the old Saturday afternoon, BBC 2 film musicals, I'd see myself on screen, the girl in the gorgeous dress, who could act like Ava Gardiner, dance like Cyd Charisse and sing, like nothing else on this earth...

When other people did not recognise this about me, it was always received with a sense of puzzlement.

In latter years I have wondered if I am akin to one of those deluded people in the Y (on earth) Factor programme – the ones they have on in the early audition stages; you know – the musical wannabes who have that implicit belief in their own amazing talent… yet we, the public, see and hear them with differently filtered eyes and ears…

Then at other times, someone will hear me, see me and praise me and I am content with my own localised stardom… for now anyway… there is still time on this earth for me to be a mega star yet or indeed to get my next fix…

And here's the thing – singing in public still takes me wildly out of my comfort zone and the sound of my own voice can either mesmerise me or make me wince… so it is my ultimate vulnerability to air my vocal chords, even… singing *Love Letters* – a song made for you, and for me, in every way…

I trust dear Song that you will take my own singing as a compliment and not a caterwaul – that's for your ears to judge. Either way I'm going to love you loads… it's a love I was born with, it's a love that's unconditional and it's most definitely a love that is symphonic and so musically real…

Yours tunefully,

Sandie Super Star xxx

PS: Dear Song, just had to let you know, that when I was on a photo shoot – with the Damsels in Success team, on a rainy day in Regents Park (July 2011), I just *had* to sing out my excitement. I started singing pretty much on arrival and soon a whole chorus of us were joining in, including in some of our group shots... When it was my turn for my solo photos, our fabulous photographer – Christina Morassi, told me that I needed a stage and so here I am – dancing barefoot on a wet park bench and absolutely loving it! Thank you, old friend xx

My park bench song and dance act
- jazz hands obligatory...

CHAPTER 4
The Skin

Summer Bradbury and me,
celebrating our birthdays in June 2010,
with Lucie providing the cake

Letter to the Skin

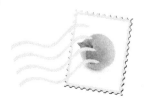

Dear Peachey Skin

As a child I never ate the skin of the peach. Its fuzzy feel felt unnatural on my tongue. So the skin had to be dealt with and there were times on long ripened fruit that the felt covering, peeled simply away, and there were times when it was harder, that it clung, and then it broke into unpleasantly small Peachey pieces that had to be worked at, that delayed the devouring, that stayed and halted the anticipated pleasure.

Then as a teen I discovered the nectarine: the smooth-skinned cousin of the peach – which replaced all that uncertain furriness with cool smoothness; which meant that all the poetic Peachey deliciousness could be dined upon instantly, with no peeling preparation to halt the wanton process of consumption. The nectarine skin could be easily eaten and so this related fruit became the posh peach – more difficult to source and more expensive to own and indulge in.

The skin of a peach is the covering, a thin protection that holds together the fruit and yet allows it to be pillaged easily, giving up its goods to the vampire who wishes to engorge on its aromatic inners. It has a mild elasticity which will easily give way to bruising, progressing easily on to moist rottenness. Its unique fuzziness tests the touch sense of the tongue – so that which I used to find challenging, now the adult me embraces as part of the Peachey experience.

The velvet wrap of Peachey skin can become a metaphor for many things. For me that goes from metaphor to mentor – to people who surround me and nurture me and allow me to be me, to grow, or to be bruised and always to bear more fruit. Just a few days into my love letter challenge I had the joy of sharing a day with two of my favourite mentors, and so, quite naturally, I wrote a *Love Letter to the Rocket Man and the Bonny Wee Lass.*

Then there was Lucie. A woman, a force of nature, a leader, a teacher and so much more - some one who has had a huge impact on this loving life of mine; so I always knew a *Letter to Lucie Bradbury* would be born. A letter charting episodes in her ways, our travels, our troubles and then our conjoined joys.

And without skin there would be no fruit – nothing to hold the physical substance together, nothing to define the form, the shape and the outcome. So too without large happenings in our lives, we too would be formless, never evolving, staid and possibly stuck, so it was that the *Letter to the Lost Lover* came about. This letter came from pain, it gave my life till now a shape; it represented long patterned history, combined with recent shattering story. And more than this, it provided a Peachey profile of an archetypal every past lover man, flowing to a point in near history, wrapped together in a safe skin, so I could gently love it and let it go. As this letter progresses, I am discarding the skin as something that is no longer wanted, so that I can see the gorgeous possibilities of a life shaped positively by, and now free, of past loves and negative consequences.

Sometimes I find the skin of the peach bland and sometimes I find that it is bitter and uncomfortable and that it sticks in my teeth – a constant reminder of a discarded piece of fruit, not letting go of its tight place, simply sticking to my gums. I never intended for it to be that way, though if I eat, if I partake of life, at some point it will be inevitable and so, somehow is loss.

My *Letter to Loss* was written six days after my mother suddenly died. The grief I experienced was forming and raging and changing its skin constantly. Then, when I touched and traced over the skin of my loss, I realised that new colours and clarities emerged, that life shifts and tilts and so emotions slide with it. These losing happenings can be life's demons or they can be life's lessons. What started out as bruising, crushing horror and anger, gave way to experience, acceptance, learning and love.

It is always time to acknowledge the friends, mentors and important happenings in all our lives: to revere them, rejoice in them and wrap ourselves in their gorgeous, fuzzy skin.

And from love, in my Peachey life, springs more letters…

Yours faithfully, always,

Sandra

Letter to The Rocket Man and The Bonny Wee Lass

Dear Richard and Liz

Well perhaps it's not quite the done thing to write a letter to someone on the very day that you see them, but then these are *my* love letters and I get to make the rules!

The thing is that I'll be seeing you today along with at least a hundred or so other people and having said that I know that I will get a hug from each of you and some words and some love, so I'm more than good with that, and those things alone would make my day worthwhile, but then there will be so much more being given and shared too.

Dear Mr Rocket Man, it has to be said that you have created something that is so fundamentally simple and yet so profound, that it has changed the lives and hearts of hundreds of people. Your 'Broadband Consciousness' is the most all inclusive school of thought that I have known in the world of self development... in your company I have met people from every walk of life, every social strata and people who wouldn't know what the phrase 'self development' meant, only that they are living freer and happier lives.

So how do I love thee? You are an uncle, a sage, a brilliant orator; there is a childlike glint of glee in those eyes, an amazing energy, a genuine desire to make a difference. Then there is the brilliant non-conformist conformity of the hair and the outfits... the Sergeant Pepper Jacket is my personal favourite. You also happen to be the life and business partner of My Bonny Wee Lass, the gorgeous Glasgow scrap, my lovely Liz.

When I met you dear Liz - my 'bonny wee lass', I realised that I could very happily earn a living making Liz-a-Like dolls – I reckon I know at least 200 people who would buy them and want to carry your image around and keep it with them too...

It all starts with the hugs, bone-crushing, loving and reviving. I have compared notes with others in the field and it has been universally agreed – you give of the very best there is!

You are beautiful in every sense of the word. You give of your love and your wisdom and your tears freely. And when I found out that you were going to teach people how to coach (and there were no boundaries – life coach/business coach/mentor), I pounced on the opportunity – it was so the right thing at the right time for me, as I started my own business and my journey as a coach in turn.

I've had the pleasure and privilege to call you my own life coach *and* my coaching mentor and to shine a light on the way forward and trusting me too to do it my way. And I've sat on your coach-ey sofa with the tissues, working through my stuff. And you have gone beyond what anyone else I know in that situation would have... in many ways, ways which are ours to know, behind our confidential client closed doors, because you give a special kind of unconditional love, one that I recognise and respond to, because I now realise I am capable of that too, and you put your trust in me and so it was.

You are an amazing judge of character and can see into someone's head and heart so easily and speak their thoughts. I've seen you meet someone new, many times and 'get' them – just like that, it's a gift.

And the love comes too from a shared loved of coaching. You know how much I love it and I *love* working with my clients – it is the most gloriously selfish, selfless thing I could ever do in my life and with my life. It just feels like I was born to it. It is energy, contentment, wisdom, electrical sparks, love and magic. In that room, with that person, all the things learned and unlearned come to me…'cosmic faxes' as Richard so wonderfully describes them…

Now to me, what you have both created is magical and I have translated it to my own philosophy of 'know yourself, love yourself, be yourself' and I will continue to sing that from the rafters… or from the stage of your Christmas party (again)… or wherever someone will listen, for that matter.

And that's my love for now. There'll be more. Can't wait for my hugs,

S xxx

Liz Ivory & Richard Wilkins –
the Rocket Man & My Bonny Wee Lassie

Letter to Lucie Bradbury

Dear Angel in Chief

That we have stayed together now through thick and thicker is a testament to our own strong wills, sometimes clashing, sometimes forgotten, sometimes celebrated...

And love can come in many ways, and shape itself to time and tide and so it can grow, and here then is *our* love story, told from *my* sandy shore...

The first time we were in a room together, we didn't meet... we were all celebrating an amazing year in someone else's company. The same someone else suggested I get in touch with you later, when I wanted to fix myself of my life's ills (or so I thought). So I came into your orbit, walking a muddy path from the life I had created towards the life to be...

Then I find myself in a room with you again, shared with other women, learning NLP – Neuro Linguistic Programming... and very scared that I would learn the keys to the universe, yet would fail to unlock the door...

My eyes were opened to training, but not as I had known it, or had indeed delivered it, in dusty corporate rooms of the past... This training room had cushions and candles, hugs and dreams, and still we learned the solid techniques of brain and language. NLP did not change my world, in some ways, but this new experience showed me that I was not a broken thing; and I realised that this knowing could be a gift that I in turn, would give to the world.

So you didn't want to send your newly trained fledglings out into the world on their own and created your fabulous feminine community… and there was I, a 'Damsel in Success', witnessing you too, stepping onto your stage, sharing the secrets of your heart's success. Teaching and inspiring and breathing deep, bringing more and more stars into your orbit. And I watched too, through my own lenses, as you stepped through your own new life stages – planning a wedding, working with women, loving and laughing and so looking forward to bringing your first baby into the world.

And very soon, I skipped to the front of the room and said, this *must* go further, we must get it out there, let me help you make it so…

I can't remember why, but we were chatting the day you went for your baby scan… we were both giddy and excited that you would see your unborn girl and get to know her better. Then the scan revealed that all was not well with the precious embryo princess swelling in your womb. The news was a blow, a time of tears. You handled it so amazingly… I watched with admiration and love while you shined through the news and loved your way forward. And since you had created a supportive sisterhood of a community, we closed in to blanket you, as you needed it, and yet still you had the love lead *us* through this too.

Then your gorgeous girl was born and we watched her stay – an angel child, a true gift of God. And she didn't have the simplest of starts, yet she survived and thrived and now toddles amongst us, testament to the love invested in her, in so many ways.

And the 'Damsels in Success' community, was your baby too and times changed and that baby needed to leave or needed to grow and so, at this time of love and expansion, when it could have sank or shrank, instead it multiplied...

Your love well invested, now paid dividends and there I was at your elbow, stepping up into the spotlight beside you and then... we fell out... of love, of synchronised vision. We attacked, we parried. Our partners duelled on our behalves... Love turned to difficulty and to the heavy weight of picking up the phone to speak words that would not heal... And I really can't speak for your side, but at this strange and changing time, I was mainly in the business of blowing smoke up your ass...

Yet through all the fog, there was still love. I *loved* your baby and would not want to let it go. All the difference had been made to my life and now it was *my* turn to shine the light. Stubbornly I clung on, I would not walk away and so I suggested ways to stay... and we started the clock again and kept on loving and moving...

And here we are now, we have both come so far, and there have still been hillocky jolts along the way, but here is the thing – when you say you love me, I feel the huge force of your heart. And it is truth and sharing, journeying and light. And of all your children, I find it strange to be the problem child at times, but you listen and I listen, and as wise women we know that the things that set us apart, sometimes are strangely the things that bring us closest together too... And in the end, as I've always said – what we create in our twin energy field, will reap wondrous rewards and glorious lessons for us both... and so it came to pass...

And who knows what stage of our journey we are at, sometimes in step and sometimes out, yet always with the same vision in soft sight.

Now when all is said and done, love is a gift and you are definitely a gift to me, my 'Angel in Chief'. Who knows where our wings will take us??? I can't wait to find out, can you?

With love from Sandie...
your 'Auntie Angel' xxx

Auntie Angel and Angel in Chief

Letter to the Lost Lover

Dear Lost Love

I waited, not always so patiently for you to come to me... Over years, over tears, over dreams. Tumbling desires, stumbling steps taken falteringly towards you. False starts, then true strides to the man, to the one, to the lover, the faithful friend, the father, the sharer.

You've worn different faces, yet the end result was the same... a heart open, a heart broken, first by me and then, squarely, by you. Loving and unloved. True love and passion and comfort and life long togetherness, blessed... But not forever blessed; tested and turned instead.

Why have you not seen me, fully? You saw me, were dazzled, then blinded... Why my lover, why is that my story, what purpose could that possibly serve?

It is not my karma to be left bereft, alone – I was born to love, born to fly. So is that my dichotomy? I cannot love *and* fly? Why not? I want it *all*. So it seems my Icarus wings melt and I fall to the sea; I bide my time, build my wings and soar skywards again and again, oh and again. Gliding, coasting, heading for supersonic space and instead falling back down to earth – grave and gravity drawn.

So I left you and left you again and then I decided there could be no more leaving... Leaving was a far greater pain than the stain of staying. So I said

I must change and change I did. I did everything to stay and then *you* turned me away... Once and then again – and I was so wounded, so rejected. So I took me to a nunnery. I stayed out of your path. I travelled to wisdom, I healed, I learned the lore of love. I listened, I prepared... I waited.

Then I started the final journey towards you, slower, waiting, calling you softly, whispering to you as I waited... Composing a symphony of love, writing a lexicon of our life. Then the time for you came closer and I started to glimpse you in odd and twisted guises... trying you, testing you, discarding and ignoring the impure pre-versions of you.

And then it was your time. And you knew me, you heard me and I waited coyly, so sure of the outcome. You had heard my music, came to my clarion call. I knew your face, your words and, as I called you with song, so you spoke to me and wooed me in song too and told me of your love, before you would speak the words, in an avatar.

So I was sure and certain – my call was answered, I knew your love words and heart promises before they were spoken. You breathed love before we cleaved. We wove, we danced, we dived, we planned. We fitted, allosterically locking into each other's lives.

My life turned on you. I depended on you for the change; we wove a fabric of family and connection, love, praise and cohesion. A ring bound our promises and committed us to our forever future.

And I was free of my former life, now part mother, part counsellor, all lover, all me – too free.

Amazing love, sparks, passion, laughter, life bound together. There is nothing on this earth that can touch that time; that time that has cost so much and yet changed so little, when all is said and done, in the final analysis and yet strangely, it changed everything...

Then just one argument, just several words played. Forgotten by me, picked on and used by you. Festered on and faltering, heart altering, shattering, trashing, destroying.

So you were not mine to keep, my lost lover, not mine to treasure, to keep forever. A rock crumbled, the footing lost, no anchor. Instead a missile, throwing me to your very own wolves, serving me up to your demons of rejection and fear and lack. You were first dazzled by me and then cruelly blind to me. Love now a four letter word... pain always a four letter word.

My heart could not hear your words. 'Why why why?' – I cried to heart-hardened ears – both yours and God's. Why? When I had waited so long for you, I had served my time, I had learned my love lessons, I was the best me I could ever be. Why? It was sheer insanity and death and grief and pain.

And life lives on, lungs still breathe, the heart in so much stiffened pain, still beats. The sun shines again and there is laughter, there is the home of your own heart, with its infinite capacity for healing and its wanting to love and keep loving. There is a wisdom learned, an ability to grow and cope and eventually to accept what passeth beyond your understanding.

Acceptance was so hard, so un-vindicated. Heaven could not wait, it seemed for me. It was a wrongdoing, a divine mistake, wantonly and cruelly created. Why? To punish, to balance, to teach? To push me back to square one, alone? For what purpose God? Why that cruel blow?

So I had to die, again, harder – to live again, more. To be more me, to shine freely and unfettered. To let you go… To create a new attachment, a thin umbilical cord, stuffed with love, letting go love, the cord getting thinner and thinner through to breaking point. We cannot ever completely be detached… you must know that…

Now it is a new year, a new me. I choose to cast my stones of intention and keep loving and moving to my light. Now lost lover, I let you go – lovingly, to your own future without me and yet carrying a piece of me with you, forever impacted, no matter how you try to eradicate.

You are lost to me and you were love to me and now you are past to me. We had our time and it was right that it was then. So no regrets. This is now, this is our tomorrow. Let's go beyond our love, let's do more, soar more, find our true freedom. We are all done now, we are good now.

So goodbye lost lover and fare thee well.

S x

Letter to Loss

Dear Loss

How complicated you are – you heinous thing – that thing which I have felt so much of in my life. And yet I call this a 'love' letter... So, dear Loss, let me explain, expand and elaborate...

I woke up this morning with a sense of creeping dread. My mother died six days ago and in another four days comes her funeral. My mother's funeral... As my senses came to, on the morning of this day, I was permeated with the weight of horror and fear. And then the vile bile of anger took me over...

Yes, anger pushed its fist into my heart, because I asked some invited people if they would come to my mother's service and there is, so far, silence... apparently no-one is coming... Then that evil, chiding voice says to me 'So... those people who share your happy existence don't give a damn about your sad times – your life is clearly a sham...'

Now in my innermost and knowing self, I realise that this voice takes over and holds you in its terrible thrall, especially at times like this; and it takes you down a long tunnel, where you stumble, blindly in the darkness and you cannot see what you actually have – which is – in daylight reality – so very much...

The fact is, if I really choose to count, there are two particular people who it is my dearest wish be there on that farewell funeral day – those being my brother and my mother's best friend. And of course, there will be more: friends, family, my mother's circle... Some to bid farewell and some to support me. And suddenly it comes back to me, in clear consciousness, what I always knew – that ten people or one hundred – if for no other reason than that is how it is, they will be the perfect ones to be there...

My own sense of significance and drama had briefly demanded more attention... Yet my mother's passing will be marked, as we – the living – need to demarcate such turning points in our lives – to focus our loss on, and provide the means to say farewell, so we can move onwards in our own living time. And for me the most compelling cause for a funeral is to celebrate a life having been lived, a life that has been part of your life. There are many ancient reasons why, even in this electronic and eclectic modern age, we practice such ceremonies around birth, marriage and death...

This limbo between time from death to funeral is extreme and emotional, it has shifted the axis of my world – so my demons come out to dance on my dreams and dine on my exposed flesh. I name and recognise these satanic creatures, and then I choose instead, to dance with the angels.

You see there I was with the expectation of attention and response. Yet I know that there are many reasons why people do not reply and do not come, and how I feel about this is my own business – it is purely my own response to what I have put out there (which is after all an invitation, not a demand) and is in no way provoked by anyone else. And then I know that so often I have a choice about how I can feel... so having wallowed in my fear and anger, I have now let it go. It is part of my process of processing what has happened; and now, at this time of writing, I am in a quiet space of reflection and acceptance that it will all be as it should. This newer, positive sense comes from the pure me, the one who chooses the path of light, not the tunnel. And verily, the dark demon of negativity still grabs me and tries to drag me down that tunnel; but I know, always, there is light at the end of it.

And we all do what we can, with what we've got... I had a thunderbolt moment about this when someone called me to offer her support and condolences... she is going through her own very tough times at the moment, and she recalled all the offers people give at these trying times... to be there if asked... to do anything for you – if asked; and the thing is, usually no one does ask... Well now, she said, she had decided to do *something*... as much as she could manage right then, which was to offer me 'a cuddle and cuppa'. And I was so touched and it was a wake-up call for me... me, who so many times has said, 'just let me know if you want anything' and then leaves it at intention... because I don't want to intrude, or I'm busy, or my own life takes over or it's not a priority.

And all these things are valid in their season... but maybe, just maybe, we could just all pause and wonder what we can do 'beyond the words', beyond our own small worlds, at times like these; and if that is sending our love and good wishes, then good... Yet, just for now, please support me in expanding my own horizons by considering the possibility of doing a *thing*, of actually paying it forward, as well as sending out a possible promise...

And I have received many such treasures in this limbo time... so much love, so much support, hugs, dinners, biscuits, transport, company and conversations. And people have created time and space to be with me... So there it all is, in reality – all in balance; and yet, still – so fleetingly, I felt neglected – when really, I am getting exactly the attention that I need... And I want to say thank you to everyone who has given to me in any and every way, in these few last days. I receive what you gift, so very gratefully.

So the emotional complications of my personality unfurl some more: triggered and exaggerated by sudden loss. I kick over the implications, then I cuddle them. I give breath to the evil and the enervating, then I can reconcile the consequences and realise that these leanings are my lessons.

It comes down to this... This is a love letter to loss. And it is a love letter in the sense that I appreciate and celebrate how this whole experience has 'opened me out', and how such trying times can, if we choose, alter us in positive and unimaginable ways. And having started with anger and tears, I realise now, with humility and clarity, just how much I actually have – even when this weird day started with me swimming through the lake of my loss. And this letter may be the ramblings of a grieving child or it will be whatever it will be to its reader and whatever that is, I am good with it...

Then this letter starts to wind down... and one of the many reasons it is addressed to 'Loss' is that my inner poet loves the alliteration of all the 'L's in a 'Love Letter to Loss'...

And so it is now, that I go from loss to love. I end this letter with a salutation to loss and all the unbidden treasures that it has given me. I do not in all honesty welcome it, yet I do intend to learn from it. And last of all, and most of all, I raise my glass – every time: to love...

Yours trustingly,

Sandra

CHAPTER 5
The Fruit

Me, with George (below) and Taz (above)

...all God's creatures ...

Letter to the Fruit

Dear Peachey Fruit

Fruit is a gift, fruit is sweetness (except for gooseberries and lime and ?), fruit is pudding, fruit is the end result of a labour of love, fruit is the product of sunshine, rain, toiling and harvesting. Fruit is fruition, a ripe promise of the richness of mother earth.

Fruit is the noun for all the sweet cultivated gatherings of nature, and here in its Peachey place – fruit is the ultimate production of the peach tree.

Soon into my creative challenge this Valentine February, it became very clear that by the very act of writing love letters, I had found more love; was drunk with the fruits of my own letters – immersing myself in them, feeling their flow, hearing their voice, sensing and re-reliving the vowels, consonants, alliteration and poetry. Thence the *Love Letter to My Love Letters* happened, with my lingering over the lessons learned, the memories revived; my writer's voice unleashed and freed at long last.

The fruits of my life... for one who has not borne the fruit of her own children, finds family too in friendships, celebrating the created 'family-ship' ties of 'friends who are family' in their dedicated letter of love, exploration and celebration of the roles we play in each other's lives.

So family and friends are our human ties, yet there

is more to this planet than *people* – there are other creatures who share this world with us, who are gifted to us, to share our separate existences. One of the many gifts, the fruit of this Peachey life, are God's creatures – or animalkind, and especially for me – catkind. Cats have been my Peachey companions since childhood, so it is only natural that there is a *Letter to God's Creatures* – charting the curiosity and love I feel for my feline friends.

And it can be that we receive the fruit of life, and it is also a truth that we are the fruit *itself* too. As a woman I sense that my birthright is to know my feminine glory and that this glory – that all women have, is a gift and that we are also the gift – the fruit of this life. *My Letter to Every Woman* explores our glory and rejoices in our (being a) gift. I create an archetype of us all to celebrate us all, and my experience of history embraces especially the western woman – who, the Dalai Lama tells us, will save the world.

Fruit – the things that we are, the things that surround us and most of all that feed us. Now dear Fruit, it is time to honour and remember you and be nourished once again via your letters of love.

Yours fruitfully

Sandra

Letter to My Love Letters

Dear Love Letters

Well my dear missives, it has been ten days and I have written ten letters so far... You are all out there, in the ether – created and thriving...

My love odyssey, my chaste challenge, has been to write a love letter every day of this month of February 2012 and already this journey has taken me in many different directions. To me that feels so right, for love shows itself in many ways and comes in many forms and as I move through this process, I realise the power of love and of letters and writing – more and more...

I can only sow the seeds and send my letters on their way. With the awesome power of the internet and public publishing, I put them out there, not even sure of the full extent of their reach. Yet I remember before the days of bullet points, texts and the world wide web – the absolute thrill, the life line, the love line of receiving a letter to me, for me alone – from family, friends and connections. There was the excitement of seeing the envelope, of recognising the handwriting and checking the wavy franked imprint covering the Queen's face on the stamp. And *stamps* – I used to collect those too as a child, loving the exotic, far away connections to the world beyond my girlish knowing, to be reached out to and discovered in times to come...

Great things came in envelopes and landed on

the mat… news, views, information, pen pals, photographs, my place at university, job offers… I remember too that I have been 'asked out' by not one, but two different men, by the medium of a letter! And there was sad news too, falling out, rejections and returns. And I remember friends sharing letters from their lives, a 'Dear John', read with tears or love letters shared with pride. Yes, I guess they were somehow slower times, that time of letters… time to consider, time to share, to re-read, to gorge yourself on words.

I used to avidly hoard my letters from lovers and from friends, with their news, emotional drama, falling in and out of love and friendship. They were so full of love and laughter. And then at some point in my life, I threw them all away… feeling that I didn't have the time or space for them, that I should not be attached to my past. Well what's done is done, but sometimes, oh sometimes I would love to trace the words again, to feel the temporal pull of the past's triumphs and turmoil… So now I write again, I recreate, I replace, I redress the balance…

So now letters are a forgotten form, little used, replaced by emails and social media. We go for speed, for neatness, for cheapness instead.

A little while ago I reconnected with an old friend lost through time and she sent me a long, lovely letter, handwritten to perfection – honest, loving and beautiful. When it landed, unbidden on my hall floor, before I even opened it, I felt the thrill again. That day at home I had a visitor who wanted my attention, yet my attention wanted the unopened letter, to devour it and spend time with it. I asked for some time alone with my letter; enough time to read it over and over, to absorb it, understand it and commit to treasuring it...

As I have started this new odyssey of letters, I have had the obsession of a new lover, wanting to spend time with you – my perfect little creations, feeling over the many facets of love and life, going into the lightness and darkness of love and where it takes you, shapes you and shadows you...

You have filled me up, you have sent me spinning into the past and stepping into my future. I feel the force of creativity, of owning myself as a writer; and with all that – the flipping coin of excitement versus fear – my joy at sharing my love, versus the vulnerability laying myself open to who knows what?

So that is love for me, today... short and sweet, eternal, beautiful, brutal and obsessive; giving, tender, fierce and gentle. So many things you are and will be... my loves... my love letters to life and to me...

Forever loving, Sandra xxx

Letter to the Friends Who are Family

Dear Friends and honorary:
(take a deep breath here...)
sisters, brothers, nieces, nephews, uncles
and aunties, etc, etc and so on...

My blood ties are few... I have a mother and a brother living, and my dear departed father provided me with a whole crowd of first cousins and through them many more seconds and thirds. Somehow though we were out of kilter with them in family history and we stay in rare Christmas card and family funeral touch... No children for me and my bro, no living grandparents, aunts or uncles or anything else and so that is our little Peachey family...

So there is me – 'friend' to a few... sometimes called sister... I always wanted a sister – ideally a twin one; there are twin girl cousins out there in the family tree; yet not me. Not quite an only child, but spaced from my big brother by nearly eight years and we were together in the early years, then separated through adolescence and distance and caught up with each other later in our lives, when our dad died.

So friend becomes sister, becomes honorary auntie to babies... this role given by friendship, affection and love extended to you, as a non-blood relative. You get to love the expansion of your friend's lives. The title is given as a gift and in return you give gifts back... as 'cool aunt' your brief is to spoil those darling children rotten when you have the ways and means at your disposal...

So you grow up and grow older, watching the babies follow in your wake, establishing the patterns of their lives... watching the changing facial features, the family characteristics – now like their mum, now like dad... grand-dad... cousin... who knows who? The inherent fascination and dissertation of seeing the lineage reflected and altered in unique genetic combination.

And as my world is filled with new generations, so too is my mother's. No blood grand-babies for her, so she becomes honorary Nanna to two. So proud I am she does this, that she is allowed to shine and show her capability for love and generosity; and when I take her round to meet my friend's babies, they all hang round her, for she has a child-like quality which pulls them in. Straight away, the purse is open, gifts are given... I remember *her* mother too giving me sixpences, and so it goes on...

In my childhood, there were aunts and uncles and they came with affection and affinity, though rarely were there parental friends around to be granted the honorary given title I have gained in abundance. So even now, after a quarter of a century of being an aunt, I am so surprised at how I am accepted, welcomed and you can see – loved by those who had no choice but to have me there, to have me to share. Now they see *me*, not 'just' Auntie, for many of them have grown out of the title now and as I am

Sandra to my lifelong friends, so now too to them...

And elsewhere, I am known as 'Auntie Sandra' to *all* the family – adults and children alike – a huge loving reminder of the affectionate part I play in their lives.

So the single girl creates a family, gets to hug the children and give them back... then time flows on and she becomes a strange new creature of honorary family-ness – a great aunt indeed!

So it was that I held one baby in my arms and looked down at her and then, so little time later, it is *her* son in his turn, in my arms... I hold this newborn personality for hours, looking down at him, held and sated with the special milky love that comes with cradling a precious new life. So in that room there is mother, grandmother and auntie, all quietly together, loving this new little lad.

Then how quickly quiet turns to toddler noise and we move on and on, inexorably, pacing through life with the newcomers beside us: sometimes stopping together, sometimes in step and sometimes continents apart; and I am woven into the fabric of their living, of their memories and mostly they come closer and some shy away; and shying away is allowed, since this is not necessarily unconditional love, but it *is* acceptance, just like I gladly accepted the gift of them into my rounded, bonded auntified kind of life...

And is it coincidence this love spills over into my vocation and how much I love my clients, those whose orbits I circle in; for as I love to be cherished, I love to cherish too and to me coaching is cherishing and loving and nurturing. Sometimes this is soft supporting love and sometimes shaking love, but throughout time I would tell those babies the hard score if that was the score that I felt; and still they love me and still we move on and wherever it is we happen to go; we always move on with love. And so it is, in love of course, that yet another letter ends.

Big love and hugs,

Auntie S xxx

Letter to God's Creatures

Dear Creatures

For all our involvement, for all the power we try to wield over this planet, mankind is, in many ways, in the minority. We share it all, this creation, this never-ending motion, with God's creatures... the beasts, the animals and the pets.

As I write this letter, my elbow is resting on the haunches of George – a cat, a named pet, a creature on loan to me, a gift from God.

At some point in its evolution, catkind left the jungle and became enmeshed in the world of man and womankind. Its descendants pounced on our vermin, kept us company, then shared their fleas and their purrs.

The domesticated cat – a recognisable cousin to its wild counterparts, now resides alongside many of us and for me that particular co-habitation started early on.

I'm told we had a cat when I was a small child, though I have only one hazy memory of this creature, called Corky, curled up on a blanket.

My solid memories start later, with the kitten bought for me when I was twelve. That was the year my brother left home... so we substituted him with another boy, my lucky black cat 'Whiskers'. The love was instant... I met a tiny ball of black fluff who was

123

curled up asleep on the living room chair, he then woke up, yawned and stretched luxuriously, found his own way in to the next room for dinner, then availed himself of the litter box. I was amazed at the confident temerity of this little creature: his self assurance, how at home he already was after just a few hours, how he knew what to do and where to go. Next I discovered that he loved to play and he loved to give and receive love... and from then on I was hooked on feline kind...

This creature immediately became part of the family unit... I discovered, unknowingly, that my father had an affinity for the feline; in fact he had a special language, reserved just for the cat, (which he in turn had absorbed from his own father) and he would compliment his companion, in fun of and homage to his own lost dad, and the cat received these blandishments with quiet, blinking gratitude.

And when I left home six years later again, I packed all my belongings away, dry-eyed and only finally cried at long last when I had to say goodbye to my creature friend; as if he some how represented all that was soft and childish in me and embodied the loss of all that I was now leaving behind me, in order to walk towards my adulthood.

I had to bide my time before I was quite grown up and static enough to have my very own cat creature. And when the time finally came, I chose another black boy, to substitute my child cat, to practise my parenting skills on, to add warmth and dimension to my life; and brought him into my new home, shared with my fiancé – a self confessed cat hater...

Now I did have his permission to bring a cat in, but he was less than impressed at his first meeting with the 'little rat'. Then without my bidding, the feline magic was worked... he gave the creature a human name (Dougal) and his affection; he realised he had a living toy, a companion, a subject of endless fascination and conversation, and so his own love story with catkind began...

I left the man and he kept the cat and a little later the next creature came into my life and so on through my time. Then there was one man later on who was made sick by my cat, so the cat went and the man stayed... for a short time... Never again I said. And never again I did.

My next cat – a large ginger tiger tom named Muttley – was a challenge. He was intelligent and self possessed and kept himself to himself. I had adopted him as an abandoned adult, so who knew his story before then? So I learned to love unconditionally, getting little in return for my food and shelter. Instead I made catkind an object of study, I read, I revised, I learned... all about their physiology, psychology and genetics, and I also studied my own boy – his body language, his voice, his ways and I gave him love by food, by shelter and by soft voice. Then over years, he returned the favours and the love and later again, when he was run over by a car and his pelvis crushed – I sobbed sadly and loudly.

He survived the experience – the treating vet telling me that these cat creatures of God have the best self healing musclo-skeletal system of all animalkind, and though his pelvis formed a new shape, the tiger returned to his habitat, changed yet intact.

And there have been more and more creature companions, and I have seen the love story happen to others, again and again... and for some it becomes a feline obsession... An endless fascination of conversation and occupation.

For me, the lure is that we are bound by love to these creatures. They come to us for food of course, but then they stay with us for love. They seek our company, they desire our affection and so it is love that ties us together. We receive their company, and are part of a primordial relationship, one that is closer to nature than to man's machinations. And at times they are domesticated pets and at times they are wild creatures and it is their very differences – between themselves and ourselves – that is part of their inherent allure.

And that for me is love. So I am now sending that love out to you – from me and from George and Taz – two of my favourite gifts and most definitely God's creatures.

Yours purringly and adoringly,
Sandra x

Letter to Every Woman

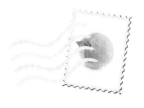

Dear Gorgeous

I am writing to you – 'Every Woman' with so much love in my heart. You, who represents all of our sisterkind, you who is every woman out there, in whatever shape, however you are dressed – body *and* soul…

What is not to love about woman? We are the miracle of this planet, we create, we care, we are the very blood in the veins of life, in every degree. Yes, man is there too and I acknowledge his role, his shape; but this is *your* letter my gorgeous goddess xxx

And I know you in so many ways, as goddess, damsel, crone, to name but a few of our flavour, our hue…

For so many of us, our lives in this modern mess of life, are a dichotomy. We always knew, throughout the millennia and the recent centuries, that behind every great man there's a great woman and slowly, in this Westernised world, our voices came out from the nursery and the kitchen sink. Then in our own mother's and grandmother's histories, man's war took the men from our hearth and we kept the home fires burning and we fed those fires and we manufactured the killing machines of war, keeping the life of our nations, turning. And still we loved and danced and made babies…

And then our free-er daughters ran free, stepping in the masculinity of sex with choice, work with trousers and the heady prizes and loneliness of leadership.

So my wonderful woman, like children we have tested our boundaries and we lived tied by kitchen sink chains for millennia and then we tried suits and swagger for our recent decades.

And yet despite all this being out there in the ether of the earth; I know I dreamed as a small child of being a beautiful damsel, waiting to be rescued by a prince on a white horse; and a field of multi-coloured horses have galloped by since... So the waiting damsel became a damsel in distress, turned bitter by lack of love and worn out from driving the wheels of the man's world of work and play.

So many of us fabulous females know this story, this dichotomy of being pulled so many ways – being bound into a life of straitened female destiny (wife, mother) *and* an endless modern male morass of choice and push (wage earner).

So many of you my sisters, have started to seek, to live, to be, to find the third way in our 'her' history, our her story, our herstory. To cherish the many millennia of our mothers and to honour our recent female forebears their trail-blazing to our modern day selves. We seek to heal, to redress and accept the many faceted female characteristics that make us, and to take them and make them our own; forming new paths in this wonderful womanly world. To transform from a 'Damsel in Distress' to a new archetype – the 'Damsel in Success'. Having our cupcake and eating it, wearing the shoes we choose, to walk down the streets, up the mountains and along the pathways where we dare to dream the way forward…

That was and is my journey, to being a Damsel in Success, to finding my way; making the path easier by knowing, loving and being myself, in all my girl glory.

I choose to be a Damsel in Success, in the form that works for me, facing life as part of the fabulous feminine-kind that I was born to and I know now – born for. Knowing myself is being woman; woman who was manmade and can be man, sometimes, when the occasion is called for… to take charge, be business-like… then back to blonde, back to girl, back to friend, back to mother…

So from me back to you – Every Woman. So many of us sisters are finding the third way now and we come together – to learn, to share, to support and to lead the way – the third way: some to trailblaze, some to shine a soft light on the world of woman *and* of man and of course of our co-creation – child…

With women's hearts, as natural creatures of love, the combined power of our feminine pulse is immense. So feel that feminine power, the strength of sisterhood, the love of many millions of good women… each one an amazing piece of nature and then nurturer of dreams, of babies, of creations and so we are back to love – again; my gorgeous, fabulous, Every Woman...

With lots of love and chocolate

S xxx

PS: As a 'Damsel in Success' I must honour and acknowledge the organised sisterhood of the same name, of which I am both member and leader. An early convert to the cause, I have the joy and privilege to work alongside its founder Lucie Bradbury and the fabulous team she has nurtured; in order to support women to live the life of their own success, with natural feminine ease. She has presented so many of us with the choice and opportunity to see and walk the third way, and my love and gratitude can know no bounds for that...

S xxx

PPS: You can find out more at:
-www.damselsinsuccess.co.uk,
where you will find your nearest group...

S x

Lucie Bradbury, my 'Angel in Chief' and the next generation of Every Woman, her daughter Summer Grace...

CHAPTER 6
The Harvest

The celebration of a sunset over Rhodes

Letter to the Harvest

Dear Peachey Harvest

Now comes the time for my Peachey harvest... to gather in my prizes, my recompense, my incentives, my crop, my yield...

Time to pluck what is mine from the Peachey tree: to salivate, swallow, share, and some too, to sell.

As I have sown, so shall I reap. And I start with the ultimate material harvest – money – a *Love Letter to Money*... Does that make me a greedy girl? Possibly, yet also an honest one, who explores, celebrates and has written this letter setting my intention for the relationship I have with money and the one that I want with money, and that I seek to garner more of this particular harvest in my life, for many reasons and seasons. I'm putting it out there: letting my head and my heart know where I want to go, creating the expectation to be returned with the harvest, setting my store, creating my vision to aspire to and then to reach.

Then there is the letter *to (a life of) Choice* – something I didn't even realise I had for oh so long in my life... so now I harvest my choice in every way – how I live and I create and how I work.

And my next letter – *to Comfort*, combines the material and the sublime, for comfort is most definitely a gorgeous harvest – one of my very favourite things – so here I dip and delve into it, search and survey it; inhaling in its inspiration, its transcendent abundance, its ability to sooth and reward and expand my soul. Comfort can be a thought or it can be a thing, and it is most definitely something to be celebrated.

There is so much celebration in these *Peachey Letters* – why not then, a *Letter to Celebration* itself? I love to celebrate, in all ways, shapes and forms, and I ponder this, as I remember the path of this love from the early times of my life, through to the now woman who loves a perfect party. And that party can be solo or it can of course, be huge. The important thing is the act, the conscious consensus of celebration.

The harvest is the purposeful integration of all the things we put into life and thus all that we receive from it too: to keep, to store and to share.

Here's to sweetly gathering in…

Yours abundantly

Sandra

Letter to Money

Dear Money

We've been through the merry-go-round together, haven't we? There have been dips, there have been peaks and *now* Money, I have changed the status of our relationship again. It took a little getting used to, didn't it – changing the rules like we did? Taking our own path and defying the rules of a whole, conventional, former life, the naysayers and the non-believers...

You've always been there for me, though at times I confess I thought you weren't really on my side... still, I have to say, that you have always come through.

Because we have an unconventional relationship, not everyone understands how it is with us... yet we have an understanding and I want you to know how I want things to be between us from now on. So here are my intentions, this will be our story – the map of our voyage and last, but not least, my love letter to you:

Money be mine...

Money come to me with ease; walk and run and dance with me on my journey through life, and in doing so, be my true and constant companion.

Money reward me for my virtues, for my passion, for my work, for the difference I make.

Money fly to me with wings and soar with me through the stratosphere as we spread our light together, you and I.

Money stay with me, abound with me and befriend me, for I am deserving of your light and you know that I am a warm, true and loyal friend.

Money be with me and I will take you on journeys near and far, enjoy you, use you well and share your gift.

And in return Money, I ask that you feed me soul and body; that you will protect me, give me security and luxury, clothe me in gorgeous gowns and house me in heaven.

For all this Money, I will honour you, I will take care of you and I will share your energy for the good of human and animal kind.

Money be mine forever and we will share the glory and celebrate the greatness.

Money be mine.

Love

Sandra xx

Letter To (a life of) Choice

Dear Sandy

I remember about a decade (or a lifetime) ago, I had a boyfriend who was a unique breed at the time... he made a living selling goods on EBay and a good living at that. He had decided to leave his high flying career in the rat race and then simply set up his own business, working from home.

Now at the time, this freedom of choice struck such a chord with me – I had just come out of relationship with another man who told me that not only could I not work part-time, as I had wanted to, for so long; but in order to get the decent house of our dreams, we would both have to work long and hard for the next 10 years... We clearly weren't compatible, but that's another story...

Now with this new man, a new way started to dawn... here was someone who had decided he wanted it his way and had created a new reality for himself... one where he would get up with his body clock (around 11.00 am), take sunny days off 'work' to sit in the garden with a book, and chose who he sold to / worked with.

Now I was good with the whole lie-in and garden thing... but to CHOOSE your customer felt distinctly strange... You see I had come from years of service to whom ever the corporate world had put in my path... the good, bad and occasionally the mad...

So the seed was sown, the possibilities were laid out before me; and still I did not see that being MY path… I had a well paid, managerial, lofty position in the corporate world… and so my fantasy slowly started to form – I would work part-time, (eventually, at some indeterminate point in the future). For – let's face it, I was just some one who could NEVER be self employed, that was beyond the realms of my capability and reality… Yet still I as I worked away, corporately, for those long and difficult hours - I was tired and stressed and frequently found myself doing things that I found completely unpleasant… oh woe was poor little princess me…

And then that man left me and so I forgot my pipe dreams and carried on with the corporate world and left those plans behind, and instead bought myself more golden ties to keep me bound into the inexorable existence that was created for me and which I only knew how to embrace.

Well dear Reader, guess how this story ends??? I left that world behind, eventually… And the changing part of the process was painful, drawn out and difficult, since although I wanted to alter my life and live my dreams; it all just seemed impossible without a future map and banks full of money firmly in place…

And so I sought support and aspiration, and STILL, over dithering months and years, I just would not commit to change. Then finally, one day, one dithering decision-less day, my mentor Lucie Bradbury - took me and bodily shook me and said

"Sandie you have just got to make the decision; just make it now and commit to it". And I wanted the words and I so needed the physical intervention to shake me out of my world and off my 'Plan A' path.

And suddenly it all became easy, the decision now made - the doors opened, my support came in and the world changed into a place of my choosing, not just of my cruising.

Now this brave new world is not all one of plain sailing, yet now I sail where I choose and I get to choose my crew mates, colleagues and clients too.

Over time, over those seas – the deliciousness of choice, of having things MY way, has become more and more desirable and indeed necessary to living my life. And it IS my way, though I sometimes share this journey and steer it with others. Some people would call THAT choice compromise and yet for me this is choice too – given freely and from my core centre – to sail, ride and walk the ways I want, with those gifted to me, on loan to me in life, to stay a short while or be there for the long distance of my life.

And my passion is to have my choice and even more as a coach, to guide others to have their cake of choice and then to eat it and to show that every one, who wants to, can bite into their own cup cake, gateau or lemon drizzle cake too.

I love that choice.

Yours choosily

Sandra x

PS: Did you know that I can chose to be Sandra, Sandy or Sandie? Any name given or transformed, by choice too...

Letter to Comfort

Dear Comfort

Well I've just got to come straight in with the compliments... what a gorgeous word you are; your beautiful cadent form is just gorgeousness personified...

What a glorious gift, what a soft, tender and giving thing you are... yes, the very thought of you makes my heart glad...

One of the many things I love about you Comfort, is the many forms you may manifest in. You can be a hug or a healing, you can be light or you can be calming, sweet darkness. Comfort is a recognised voice, a sense of familiarity and of a knowing.

Comfort too can be a hot drink, a glass of wine, a chunk of chocolate... the kiss of loving, warming food. Comfort food... mmmmmmmm... A comfort of sausage and mash wrapped in a gravy of oniony flavour; or of pure cold ice cream caressing the tongue and the throat, melting into sensory pleasure. A treasure of taste to be savoured and devoured, inhaled and duly digested.

I say, so sincerely Comfort, that I'm very sorry that I am not always faithful to you and am sometimes forgetful of you... I will often toil and trade and treat you like an affair, a guilty pleasure kept secretly for free and forgotten days, when really you are a necessity – my true love, my joy and my ultimate sanity. At those forgetful, regretful times, I push through life, I thrust and force, I cajole and cry. These are hard things to do my dear Comfort, and yet so often I do them to myself, being my own willing victim, enslaving myself to time, to effort and to (non-comforting) reward.

Now there's the thing – is comfort a reward or a right? Is it a luxury or a necessity? Is it a guilt or a given? Is it rebellion or heaven?

Comfort is love, in many faceted forms and love is my birthright, so Comfort be mine and let me be true to you. Ah Comfort, how shall I celebrate you? Simply or in a spa? I shall take you and make you in all guises and remember to wrap you around me, to share you, to prioritise you, to eulogise you, to practise you frequently and blissfully. Oh Comfort what shall we do? Let's make 'love' (and yes that can be a comfort too!)

And your form can be gorgeously simple and shape you into new names… here is one of my very favourites… I shall breathe this gently… the breath of a 'blankie', yes, the very caress of comfort enveloping me, making the corporeal me less real. Softness defined into a loving square of comfort and joy, of pride and possession, my very own selfish delight, wrapping and binding me as a gift. Draped and shaped around me, a new me, yielding and melting and slowed… ah Comfort.

Comfort be my very own, engaging my senses with ease and grace and gratitude. Comfort be long,

Comfort be often, and Comfort be continual.

Comfort be there in the fabric of my being, not sought after when I am sore or tired or lost; for with you there, as my constant companion, there will be more light and less loss, more energy, more fun and more lingering, yellow sun.

Comfort is complete and utter surrender to a yummy moment of love, an act of complete submissive tenderness; so seek comfort in your surroundings – take yourself to where comfort resides and call it to you, lure it in with love, love for yourself, for your life, for this cradled, cosseted moment. The moment of heart's ease, this single eternity of forgetfulness for everything except this delicious, comforting now.

And what is comfort? Comfort is a thousand things and it is one thing. It is various and it is simple. It is common and it is golden. It can be resting your head on a cat's purring form, paddling in the sea, listening to beautiful music: lifting you up, resting you down, flattening out the undulations and tribulations of life, filling you up, filling your senses with nonsensical, whimsical joy. Comfort, you are relaxation, slow tempo, warmth or coolness, gravity geared or stillness.

Comfort you are the very realisation and personification of slow joy; a gift, a treasure, a genuine pleasure.

Ah Comfort, I love you and that you love me too is incontrovertible, for you always welcome me in with hugging, open arms and so too now, my dearest one, I'll embrace you. Yes, here is my commitment – to comfort and to love.

Yours sweetly and softly...

S xx

Letter to Celebration

Dear Celebration

You I have always loved... in quietness, in gratitude, in the multitude of a crowd, in the pleasure of a twosome, in a knot of girl friends... on the sofa alone, on a Friday evening, celebrating the end of the week, with a curry, with wine and my favourite TV programme on standby...

I love the very thought of celebration – the preparation, the joy of creating an occasion to come; a coming together to love, to laugh, to eat, to dance, to watch, to share... to whatever it is that that we are celebrating. You I have always loved...

As a child I remember a smartie-covered birthday cake with particular joy... Ah that ritual too, that we teach to our young: to bring the cake to you – the celebrated one, to blow out the candles to applause; to wish, to laugh – then be sang 'Happy Birthday' to... How many billions of times has that celebration song been sung? Sung to so many ages, to so many shining faces reflected in the candlelight? All those songs, smiles and candles coming together, across so many years, across so many corners of the globe, sung to babies, sung to oldies, sung to tag and celebrate special tide-marked years in our own creation – this birthday ritual is a celebration of life that we are all part of, in unison... And a cupcake with one pink candle in it is a celebration and your favourite slice of Victoria sponge on an 'un-special' week day is a savoured celebration too.

And I cannot always wait to be the subject of the celebration, so I seek to create my own festivities – I mark the days, I make the arrangements. My natural born impatience never lets me miss this, even if sometimes it is just quietly with my family, as sometimes, even I, who loves the limelight – shuns the limelight; and so it is perfect for me that my family are there – as they were always there, reflecting me and celebrating and demarcating my existence in their existence. It is a family ritual, in our tiny genetic family of three, that we always come together on these birthday anniversaries.

Lest I neglect you dear friend, I seek to embrace you at all times, to see your possibilities in the everyday, in the simplest of coming togethers. And if not cake, then food is so often part of even these tiny rituals. To treat – to eat out. To be cooked for and treasured. To create a meal for those who come into the orbit of my home – to celebrate them, to nourish them, to bring them to me. To always celebrate.

So celebration is gratitude too: savouring a little carnival moment, raising my vibration with the gifts of all I have, all I am and all I do; and joining in with the gala days, hours and seconds of those around me, in body and electronically. I love to 'ye-ay' and 'hurrah' and employ the exclamation marks of joy! I end every day with a litany of all I have to be grateful for – the situations, the gifts, the people, the compliments, the lessons learned, the sunshine, the rain and sometimes the pain that shapes me to here, to now, to this single point of celebration, this current breath, this life that is the celebration of my own creation.

I choose to think in terms of celebration: to relish it, to seek it, to see its possibilities. I choose to create celebrations tiny and celebrations huge and the panoply of all in between too. I want to see celebration in my everyday existence... and when my head seeks to chide and criticise (and it does all that still – so often), then I can pause and say to myself – what am I grateful for right now, what can I choose to celebrate in this moment, on this day? And so often the chiding demons continue to conceal, and so I continue to count my blessings and this is how I move, I vote to change those dark criticisms into enlightened celebrations...

As a coach too, for me, my role is to celebrate those who come to me for direction, for support, for illumination. And I will shine the light on their gifts and gratitudes and remind them just how amazing they truly are too, these celebratory creations sent to me. Every coaching in itself is an act of celebration and for that I speak as someone who is still coached myself; so in turn I turn to those who show me that my reflection is praise and that I am understood and hurrahed and of course celebrated into different, more difficult directions when warranted too. So some celebrations are sometimes tougher roads to travel, yet always worth it when you know that celebration enervates, raises and ultimately gains you to glory.

You I have always loved, Celebration, and all my *Love Letters to Life* are celebrant acts: they all bring you along, weave you in and out of the silken fabric of my being, of my creations… all of which, in turn, are of course, celebrations.

This then is the ending of my celebration of Celebration…

Ye-ay, hurrah, woo hoo and lots of love to you!

S xxx

CHAPTER 7
The Juice

Me on holiday in Milan, about to discover the
phenomena of the Bellini

Letter to the Juice

Dear Peachey Juice

A few years ago on a short break to Milan (in Italy), I sat down in a bar next to the Navigli canal. The canal also named that part of the city, which I discovered, is a fabulous place where restaurants and bars line the waterway and the whole area really comes alive at night with happy hordes enjoying the shimmering summer ambience.

Looking at the cocktail menu I was intrigued to see a Bellini – a concoction of peach purée and prosecco… Hmmmm… Just the thought of combining two such gorgeous ingredients was an enticing one. So it was that my heightened expectations were in no way disappointed when I tasted the gently sparkling white wine prosecco, tinctured a delicate creamy peach, with the aromatic, sweetly tart crispness of the fruit's fresh juice and flesh – all intermingled to divinity.

Bellini… the very word is a singular poem and now, to me, it was a sumptuous drink that captured the essence, the sweetness and continental luxuriousness of that whole Italian experience.

To make a Bellini requires squeezing the juice out of the peach, making the most of it, capturing its essence, marrying it with another special element, so to enrich, elucidate and enhance. And the same holds true of the Peachey life – to squeeze the full juice out of it, to experience it in full, to consciously decide how to create and live it so it can be the most fulfilling, giving, enjoyable, exciting, supportive, varied, musical, quiet and comforting life on any given day and many more such epithets on any other given day in this span of existence.

To start with, you must set out your stall and create your intentions, so that the universe and your psyche can collaborate; and so, together, you set in motion and realise your desires, dreams and goals. Ready the glass, so that the Bellini can be poured into it… Thus is written my *Letter to the One* – my once and future lover. And in writing it, I can already live the experience, bathe in it, relish it and be ready for it.

For *me*, squeezing the juice should not be a labour, since it could be said that work is that hard part of my life that exists simply to provide the juice to fund it. How would it be instead if work *was* the juice, part of the delicious concoction of my existence? Hence this is my consideration in my *Letter to Work* – finding the love, mixing it all into my Bellini living.

If there is a method to my Peachey madness, could there then be madness in my methods? My *Letter to Coaching* opens the toolbox of my craft and lovingly looks at the implements, the components and the interweaving of my innate capabilities, my learned lessons, my lifetime of experience, and how only I can provide this singular spectrum of support. Pulsing and blending all the elements of this peach, into a one and only bespoke cocktail.

I am a social creature: I love to support, to share, to impact. If work is love, then it must follow that the people I share that time with – are loved too. It feels like strange territory to think of clients in these terms – a lifetime of work ethics disengage and reformulate; and in doing so, most definitely and deliciously flavour the outcome... and so happens my *Letter to My Clients*.

To squeeze the juice, is to taste the results, so I set the glass before you and start to pour... Cheers!

Yours juicily (of course...)

Sandra

Letter To the One

Dear You

Today is Valentine's Day, that ultimate day of declared love, and so I'm thinking about you and I'm waiting for you … patiently at the moment as it happens. That's rare for me … patience is a virtue that's definitely in development for me a lot of the time. But right here, right now, I'm being good and patient. I'm just scanning the horizon softly, biding my time.

At other times I long to see you and start our time together, but it's OK that it's not now. It will happen when the time is just right.

It will be so worth the wait. You will be amazed at just how good it is. My love is good, it's like nothing you will ever have known and I have yet to discover how your love will look, feel, sound, smell and taste in every dimension of our being together. I'm so looking forward to unchartered voyages of discovery, revelation and laughter.

As humans we are given the gift of love … there is the physical realm – affection and ties that bind us together so we support and survive and there is also passion – the life force, pushing us to pleasure and procreation. Next there is the realm of being seen deeply, of finding a kindred spirit, of feeling part of something bigger than yourself, being recognised and reflected back in all your glory. There is simple togetherness, rubbing along as a couple, facing the day in company, a thousand million words and silences; touches and flashes.

But then I have known love, a lot of it. The word has been said to me and at me and by me, so many times. I used to guard what I gave, I was spikey and defensive, because I felt I had been unfairly attacked by it in the past. Then I decided to change, to open my heart and give freely and in the flow. Now as a tactic, neither of these paths seemed to lead me to any where in particular, except perhaps towards heart break or inertia, but that is the past, my Mr One and now it is time to move on. It is up to us now to create a new époque, one that is grand and quiet and which sweeps away the hurt past and sees our many lessons in love as our future joys.

Where shall we move on to you and I? I sense it now, glimpse our time together – these future memories which will be ours and ours alone.

How will that love be, between you and me? It will be what it will be, that is our little secret for tomorrow, when our time becomes today.

Do I dare to call you 'soul mate'? Several times already in this life I have had those words uttered to me, so I'm guessing I'm allowed more than one soul connection! Such a label doesn't matter to me my Mr One, because we will write our own book of life and of love.

Will we have a different kind of love? I really

believe that you cannot love two different people in the same way, so that will have its own perfect consequences for us and so I can move to you, new, free and unfettered; surrendered and sure.

It's nearly the end of another Valentine's day and I faced the day happily. I have given and shared love, I have celebrated; I have walked the woven fabric of my life and I am contentedly biding my time. For the time will come, OUR time - that's a simple fact, a knowing for me. So I will prepare myself well and be as realistically ready as I can be, in body and heart.

I'm loving you already and I'm so looking forward to you, my Mr One.

Happy Valentine's Day darling.

With so much love,

S xx

Letter to Work

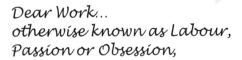

Dear Work...
otherwise known as Labour,
Passion or Obsession,

I remember years ago when I was a child, my mother buying a postcard with the phrase 'Work is a Four Letter Word' printed on it and taking it into her own place of work... I don't know what response it got or if her boss ever saw it... and the whole 'four letter word' thing passed by my childish understanding until later life...

I started off my working life as a babysitter, passed teenage Saturdays and holidays cleaning and shop assisting and after the high expectations of university, my first foray into the big, adult world of work was selling photocopiers. God – how I hated plodding round industrial estates asking for compliment slips, knocking on doors, getting rained on and rejected. And still I sold more than all the men who worked in the office with me...

Though eventually I got 'the sack' for taking time off 'sick', because it made me so miserable... And that seemed to be the first in a long line of sabotage tactics that would get me out of 'jail' fast and supposedly free.

I have had jobs since then that have made me so miserable that I would groan as soon as I woke up, knowing what I had to face that day... horrible tasks and nasty people, sucking out my soul, all in the cause of work and pay. I stopped, started and moved around in my twenties, until I fixed on a 'career' in human resources and unwittingly became a manager – and that not even by choice. I was working at the time as a HR officer in a dark little office in a factory somewhere and thought I might just be there forever. Then one day I got a call from a 'head hunter' and was chased and flattered into a situation where overnight I doubled my salary, status and stress and became a career girl.

Well dear friend, you changed your name from 'work' to 'career' and we had a real love/hate thing going didn't we? I loved the sense of importance, the drama, the sparks I could create and the difference I made. I was the object of respect, lust and puzzlement on production lines and in offices. I adored the company cars and all the other trappings of corporate reward; including working lunches and trips abroad – even when most of my colleagues were men in grey suits. I loved dressing the part in my own smart little suits. And there is the camaraderie of work, I have always loved that and made some very close friends as a result.

I climbed higher and higher up the corporate ladder, yet hated taking other people's flack and working insane hours with no thanks. Then there was being one boss's favourite and another boss's nemesis, and often I would start off as the favourite and some how end up as the nemesis – sabotage unconsciously 'saving' me and then pitching me back into a new lion's mouth. And more and more I was the agent of the corporate machine, making people redundant and acting like an undercover policewoman out to catch them in deceit and wrongdoings. That made me miserable.

I wanted to make the change, but didn't know to what. I just couldn't think outside the treadmill, the responsibilities I had created in this life and any alternatives just seemed unfeasible. As the years passed I felt more and more jaded, burned out, broken and incomplete and *had* to start my journey to the light, to living my truth, though I couldn't see the direction and threw away several torches to it along the way.

So I went on courses to 'fix' me and spent time with people who nurtured me and who were walking a path I dared to dream to follow. Then I realised I wasn't actually broken and that all this 'stuff' I was putting into me, would be an amazing gift to share...

And suddenly an opportunity came to me to combine my years in human resources and my coaching skills – my own unique life combination – to help 200 people facing redundancy find new work, change careers and face new futures. I felt passionate about supporting every single person in my care, even if it meant swimming across raging rivers to get them to where they wanted to be. Wow – career turned to passion!

Then came my own business, which sometimes succumbs to the name 'obsession'. I lead, I coach, I train, I mentor, I make a difference to individuals and companies and all the time speaking my truth, doing it in the only way that I can. I am my own sum total, a fabulous confluence of skills and experiences that I pour into my life and the lives of others entrusted and entrusting to me. I love, I give, I challenge, I stretch, I support and I laugh. And I cry sometimes too…

This isn't work, this is life and this is love. And you *know* how much I love Love!

Happily yours

Sandie x

Call that work? Me in action…

Letter to Coaching

Dear Peachey Coaching

I was feeling that familiar weirdness that comes to me when I start some of these letters... A jarring sense of addressing a *thing*, a *phenomenon*, in a way that I usually don't, in my even plane of sane, daily, practical living... So somehow addressing this letter to 'Peachey Coaching' felt easier – *now* it is not a treatise of a 'professional' person; instead it is a voyage through what I invoke and employ – the unique blend of elements that I call upon and am always developing, to be a Peachey Coach.

The *desire* to *be* a coach came first... For so long I told myself that I could not coach because I did not have a certificate that said I could; an important piece of paper that proved that I had proved that I could indeed coach.

But then I had forgotten about a Peachey lifetime of experience as a human resources manager in the corporate world; a world where I would solve, troubleshoot, sooth, challenge, create, explain and frequently... coach – coaching just wasn't a label I applied to what I was doing back then...

In my now and blended life, I still love to work in the corporate world and thus coaching blends seamlessly more and more into what I do in that orbit. I am known as coach outside that sphere too (going by labels of business coach and life coach) and wherever I am coaching, whether it is in an office, on my sofa, on the phone, or on a park bench… the processes are the same – to support someone to wanted changes and to desired outcomes; to bring out their best; capitalise on their strengths; support them in recognising and clearing blockages; shining a light on what can not always be clearly seen with our very own eyes – and so often elucidating and reflecting to them that they *are* the light …

I am educated, trained and of course, well read in many tools, methodologies and techniques. So what happens if I open my coaching toolbox – what is in there, exactly?

I remember starting my training in NLP – Neuro Linguistic Programming – a set of teachings and techniques which seek to wreak change. On the precipice of learning I was scared… What if this offered me the keys to the world and I failed to turn the key in the lock? I studied and I practised and I observed and as I came to the end of my training nearly two years later, there had been a sea of change, and now I was happy that I was enough: that experience had shown me that whatever was needed, whenever I sat opposite a new client, would come to me. That I could trust… myself and the client, so that together we can create desirable outcomes.

I am enough… and I am a lot as it happens… And so much gets downloaded to me in a coaching session – things come in that so often I didn't even know I had consciously stored. My natural support inclinations combine with training and consciousness. Training in how to question, calibrate and develop. A genuine desire to enable people to realise their full and true potential, with ways to stroke and sometimes shake it into their realisation, into their being and doing selves.

At one point, not so long ago, I turned my back on the corporate world for a wee while, as I re-invented myself as a 'Life Coach', and so it was that I was going to save the world one 'om' at a time... Yet the corporate world and the business world drew me back in... Where else would twenty plus years of working wisdom go?

One of my favourite tools of corporate life – the psychometric toolbox, particularly pulled me back into my corporate suit (now a red dress as it happens). As a people watcher and amateur psychologist from childhood onwards, the adult me loves wielding this weighty tool to inform decisions, commence coaching relationships and teach both the similarities and differences in human behaviour – that explain, that bridge and that bring about improved communication and positive changes.

So those are some of the hard tack tools... how about a natural propensity for love, support and caring? A genuine desire to gain results and see your clients move forward in baby steps and giant leaps.

And sometimes it simply feels bigger than me... whatever your belief system, you can call on support and will receive downloads outside the conscious mind if you ask for and are open to the answers.

Feel this with intuition, with God-given advice, or if you choose connect to your higher self or ask your subconscious – I admit to all of these and they all supply me well, in their smart order.

Always before being with the client in appointed time, there is a prayer – the preparation, the invocation to serve them, to support them in whatever ways will best feed their purpose. And this coaching process: before, during and after, is the greatest energiser for me – it is an alchemic coming together of what is within and without me, concentrated to this coaching point, this coming together with a client.

And the *satisfaction* I get from coaching… well what I experience is beyond that… Of seeing others getting release and result… I cannot describe those sensations here, for this is beyond my words. In a cliché I can say that it is a genuine privilege to be in a position to do this; so this cliché will have to serve, for that is what it is and that is what I do.

So that is my lore and my skill, and what I do in the coaching context. It is the blend of empirical and inspirational that comes together, to form what only I can provide. The blend that can only be mixed and provided by me: the sum total of all I am, channelled into 'Sandra Peachey – Coach': a Peachey coach no less and yes, also infinitely more… as being coached too, myself – constantly reveals to me …

Yours sincerely

Sandra Peachey

Letter to My Clients

Dear Eleanor and Sean

It doesn't seem quite right to call you client or customer or consumer; or even punter, coachee, mentee, student... So I warm to you as named beings, representing the sense of how we relate in this crazy and amazing existence we co-inhabit.

Here is my love letter to you and I falter at the beginning, because even now it seems odd to say 'love letter', here in this complicated context... but then again, it is so right too... so let's explore that...

First of all you know always, that I chose to be with you, as you chose to be with me – to step forward together, to figure out the ways, the routes and the senses of your journey. So I am there to support, to challenge, to advocate, to fuel your propulsion forward. Sometimes to teach, oft times to facilitate; always to share, to show my way and in doing that, shining a light on *your* way.

So how is it that I can say that I 'love' you...? As I explore the many facets of love, I discover more and more that each love I have in this life of mine is in itself a multi-faceted, variously fractal and gloriously complex thing.

And you can dare to love, acknowledge the love you have around you and allow it to take its form in every aspect and yes... I digress... from you – Eleanor and Sean, meandering back to the very subject of love itself, again.

So to you I say our relationship is one composed of many elements... wisdom, love, advice, magic, learning, energy, vision, talent and... well the list is infinite and it is composed of the elements of who I am and who you are... So in fact there are many lists... Who I am in this context is an ever-evolving creature made up of my predispositions for connection, communication, pragmatism and result. To be fulfilled I really want to see, hear, feel and know that I am making a difference, creating an impact, so that you, in your turn do the very same...

So I give you the benefit of my own doubts, my experience, my skills and my knowledge; not to replicate, yet to create – for you have reached this point with all your own amazing specialities. Your uniqueness may be known to you, yet how do you get it out there? You may have a sense of who you are and crave to have that concreted, to see it, visible in front of you. Could it be for you that you see the mountain top and seek the way up there? Every one of you has a mixture of needs, composed of the practical, the task must dos, and then again also the irrational, emotional, inspirational elements that once explored, will take you beyond... beyond where you are now. And it is the 'beyond' that brings you to me.

So how does this work between you and me? There is the solid... my knowing, my imparting the material, tangible and specific. There are decades of achievements, downfalls and groundbreaking products. I was an important player in the corporate sphere... so I have all that 'big world' background and so where it is necessary, that comes in to what we do together – you and I. For as I thought one day, not so long ago, that I would walk away from it and on to a life of 'om' and pure inspiration instead, there was still a regret at leaving it behind me...

So too then I fire up your inspiration, for this is also the path I have trodden, and I have grappled with the odds that these contrasting elements bring to my life, but then that is the dichotomy of life and of work... so often I've seen you struggle with this too. But then when you sit back and ponder, of course we cannot really separate it all out... since all these elements blend together to make the one life that we have, right here and right now. How often do you see that – see people putting different parts of their lives in different boxes? Well yes, they all have their own place, their own time and appropriateness, yet so too are they all chemically bound and when I realised this, so much became so much clearer and that will be your clear vision too.

So together in our space we create magic, sparks, products, realisations, light and whatever is wanted, so we can flow freely forward. So too we traject the obstacles, see things for what they are, see them and feel them differently, explode them or climb them or even dance around them.

And I have to acknowledge *your* part in my own journey, you give me so much... you reflect, you stretch, you elucidate, you cliché complete me...

At times I feel your frustrations, your energetic obstructions and I celebrate them with you, as I know these are the things that have brought you to me, as has too your need to change and grow, along with your sense of being – to be aired, to be moved, to go to who knows where?

I'm so glad you come to me, to let me be me, to be who I am, so you can go where you want to, to realise yourself. For this is the fascination… it's all there – to be drawn and then drawn upon, in you… we are all deep wells, endless pools of knowing, skill and wisdom. Each one different, each one presenting to the world only what we can give it – our very own product, to give, to share, to sell. An exchanged energy that gives to us both – your investment, my return and in our twin orbit, only we can create that perfect picture.

So thank you for taking flight with me, for trusting in me, for knowing this is the right connection. I am humble and grateful to serve you, to walk with you, to laugh and yes, sometimes to cry and sometimes to shake you… and that is love and it always comes back to that, when we know it, in whatever way we dare and treasure to shape it.

Yes, I dare speak that word, in this relationship of ours and so that is truly love – for you *and* for me. Indeed it will be 'peach perfect for me' and whatever name that love is for you, so shall it be.

With warmest regards

Sandra, San, Sandie, Miss?

CHAPTER 8
The Peachey Tree

Me aged about three... who knew what life had
in store?

Letter to the Peachey Tree

Dear Peachey Tree

Now I have tested and sampled of this delicious fruit, it is time to climb the tree – time to reconcile and contemplate the infrastructure, the surroundings and the bare beginnings of a *Peachey Life in Letters.*

The tree gives shade and shelter, it sways in the sun, takes from the soil, it drinks of the rain and then – preceded by blossom, we gain the glorious peach in return, brought to us as a gift of nature, a true nurturing edible treasure.

It is time to trace the tree – the interweaving elements of magic that bring our lives together, that give us the view from the top, to see all, to know all and make sense of all and then to enjoy the sumptuous shade.

On this tree the first branch is the *Letter to Me.* A missive to my ego: celebrating the one and only version you will ever find, ever know, or even encounter – in some physical or metaphysical way, of this sole entity that is me, I, this Sandra Peachey. Daring to bare who I am, who I was and who I may be – in my own perceptions; the many forms and shapes I take, the quest I am on, the reflections I have seen in other's eyes and ears and words. How strange and yet how natural to trace this territory – to fight the nagging voice of doubt and so to simply find your self.

And then of course to love ... T*he Letter to Love*, the very heart of *all* of these letters: the source, the nutrients, the spine and the spirit of motivation, that ticks through them all: caressing and guiding and urging them into being and into belief. Discovering the many facets of love and how it flows into and moulds everything. Sometimes it is known, sometimes unseen, yet always there, the force in this Peachey Life.

And in the orchard are other trees, there is always more fruit and so many more possibilities; and hence comes my *Letter to a book called 'Sacred Paths Entwined'* – and to its authoress – a friend, a soul-sister – shaking her tree too. The gifts of the orchard are delved into, the crisscross prospects of yet more fruit, of different fruit, seeking more seeds, seeing more opportunities; the story of a friendship, the witnessing of more fruit nurtured and harvested from the tree, a vision of a message, of a missive, indeed of a mission, now realised.

And in the final analysis, sitting in the shade and shelter of the tree, I contemplate life itself... A *Letter to Life*: the thought of writing it both thrilled and scared me. How could I do this true justice and cover the boundaries of this boundless concept? In sailing through the waters of this living entity, do I have to contemplate death too – life's counterpoint?

In some deeper sense I knew how it would go, but could not plan the path – the journey is just too long. So I do what I have always done since I started this process of being a letter writer – I ask the questions,

I start scribing and then the answers come, the themes arrive, the sense creates itself, and so the words whirl from thought to finger. Beyond me, the letter knows its own way, and thus my thoughts and feelings are gathered together, into this act of Peachey poetry; the literacy of my letters, yes the very litany of my letters; and so it is and it was, that the *Letter to Life* was born and then was done.

Climbing my tree, there is a heady view from the swaying top, a gorgeous vista of a chunk of this physical planet – my view. My views are there too, my contemplations, my deliberations and reflections, colouring the horizon and expanding it beyond my eyes. I have tilled the soil, sown the seeds, watered the saplings and now it is time to grow, to press towards the sun, to stretch upwards and outwards in a perfect arc of trunk and branch and leaf and the fabulous notions of more blossom and fruit, a rich harvest to take from, to share and to give away.

And after the happy toil, comes the gorgeous rest: sitting in the shade, giving my gratitude, checking the concepts, planning the next harvest and so – on and on, into the sunset. Picture me, leaning on my Peachey tree – the product of me, and me too of the tree; the bark, the sap, the branches, the form that makes the fruit: the fruit that is the ultimate Peachey prize...

And all this is taken and made into *'Peachey Letters – my Love Letters to Life'* and so now, sample the tree, from me, with love (of course).

Yours truly

Sandra Peachey

Letter to Me

Dear Me

Well this one – the letter to Me, feels in so many ways like the hardest letter to write... Should this letter be first in the order of things or last – it is both... alpha *and* omega...

Where to start? How about before the beginning... I've got a real sense that I wanted to come into this life... that I chose to be born, that I jumped up into the universal ether and said 'me, me, me please!' And yet how many times in my life did I wish that I had never been born... Yes... so much emotional pain, so many tears; and then again how much love and laughter has there been?

What can I tell myself here? That it is all perfect, that it is bonkers, that it is beautiful to be me...

And I wonder how I reached where I am and then I look back at the tidemarks in my life. And always it comes back to this – one hot summer day, a six year old me ran across the road to get an ice cream from the 'ne nah' van, and the man in the van misheard me and gave me a lolly instead. And when I ran back, crossing the road, I was knocked down by a car and never got to eat my treat. Now all things considered it wasn't so serious and soon I walked and ate ice cream again; but I still bear scars from that day to this day, and part of me has often wondered if I have *ever* got over the habit of looking the wrong way and getting crushed as a result...

And on the path to adulthood there have been bullyings and beatings and there have been swings and roundabouts. And I remember sunshine and laughter too, I remember family and friends and seaside happiness. I remember pets, dresses, love and arguments all mixed in to the melee of my memory. The path to me, always being me, always now. Yet so often wanting tomorrow, wanting the day to be different, the place to be different, to be with different people; yes, hankering constantly to be away from me, today...

So dear Me, what defines me now? My nature, my nurture, my memories, my life's search, my research – to me? They all play their part. I was born with blue eyes – nurture and life's literal happenings have never changed that. I am naturally influenced by the people I grew up alongside, walking this path through our lives, sometimes in slow motion and sometimes in quick step. My memory fluctuates – much of my childhood has disappeared into a vacuum... I try to remember landmark birthdays... strangely gone, void... yet still – here I am. And always there were choices, whether I knew that at the time or not... And I chose and then I chose again and so I chose to be me.

So how would you describe, label or define Sandra Peachey: daughter, sister, friend, cousin, aunt, niece, Miss, Ms, colleague, boss, teacher, coach, goddess, sex kitten, author, dancer, actor, artist, singer, girlfriend, mother (to be), wife (to be), human resources manager, shop assistant, cleaner, cat lover, siren, muse, housewife, gourmet, chef, joker, lover, leader, Queen of Support, Circe, Cassie, Sandy, Sandie, San, dogbreath, Peaches, bitch, angel, saviour, role model, nemesis, babe, babes, bab… the list could quite possibly be endless. What a fabulous, never-ending lexicon of my life, of me… and where will the list go on to?

And these labels are opinions, are subjectivities, are passing thoughts… Who am I really? I am love, I am creativity, I am giver and nurturer, I am laughter, I am the gravitational pull that guides people into their own true orbit, into their own beauty and light. You may or may not really see me or hear me, yet that doesn't matter. I will be visible where I need to be. But if you *do* see me, then you will *feel* me too.

There have been ups and downs, there have been past regrets. Yet no 'now' regrets, for all that has happened has led to me now, and where else could I be? Who else could I be? I chose constantly, I live free, I create, I prescribe, I revive. I was born blonde and I stayed blonde; accident prone and lovable; clever and loquacious; attractive and sensitive: me, me, all me.

Now as a love letter, where does the love come in to all this, dear Me? Well as it happens, I was definitely born to love: to give love, to receive it, to spread it, to write about it, to be it. And the hardest thing, so often, is to love myself. Yet love myself I do: I must, for from that springs the rest – of that comes the best, of me. And my letters are not just love, they are catharsis and celebration too and so I dare praise myself, just as so often, I have chided myself – yet now is always the time to rejoice!

And my letters are gratitude – so I give immense thanks for those who are in this theatre of my life – in the audience and on the stage. I have toddled, walked, crawled, danced and run through my life with a whole cast of characters: some have stayed, many have gone; and the acts have moved on and the scenery has changed, and who knows where the plot will end. I feel there *must* be rapturous applause at the curtain call, for after all – being me deserves that – doesn't it?

So dear Me – I applaud you/me! Here's your standing ovation – your love letter, your magnum opus. My love in a letter, my life in a letter –

Dear Me, that *is* me… for now… There'll be more…

Forever yours,

Sandra xx

Letter to Love

Dear Love

So here we are – together, quietly, with everything in place. And because I'm sort of stubborn, this letter nearly didn't happen, simply because someone said to me 'and of course if you are writing love letters, you'll write a letter to Love...' Now see, these are my love letters and I get to make up the rules... but anyway, yes, here indeed it is, and no, I did *not* write it on Valentines Day... I had my own original plans for that, so there...

So... awkward pause again... here we are... And what to say, how to start? Well the starting is the thing with love isn't it? It can crop up unexpected, unbidden and suddenly shake your world or then again it can creep up on you and slowly envelop you, falling softly like a feather out of the sky.

And it can start as a glance, a realisation, a declaration; something known, on the tip of the tongue, at the back of the brain, from the bottom of the heart... And love comes in many shapes and shades and forms itself in solidarity or as shimmering waves.

So it's not surprising then that we do not always see it in our space. But spend a little time with love and you realise how much of it is around, when so often we are strangely preoccupied with how little we have in our lives. Yet love is an abundance – when you consider it in its every kind. Start with the old cliché of loving yourself – the very best place to start

I would say. For me that is a waxing and waning; and far from loving myself, sometimes I can be my own worst hated enemy. Yet it is the starting place of all our loves, so we must take care of loving ourselves.

Pay that first love its due, treat it with affection, shine a light on it and show yourself that you are loved. And the easiest way is to be kind to yourself, do not silently chide or scold you and don't listen to the dark voice that tells you that you cannot… be loved… instead love yourself.

And it reaches out, this love – to those around us, born to us, sent to us by fate as friends, chosen, gifted, sought. So if we are not healed and solid in our own hearts, how can we reach out for more and give of our own best love?

For love moves and grows and can also stay unfettered in our being, unacknowledged for those around us, not named, when it should be praised and thanked and explored. Well I'm biased in this of course, for these very letters are a gratitude of love, an exploration, a voyage through it. And to my surprise they were largely unchartered waters and so I simply trusted and sailed them, sometimes through choppy waters and sometimes through calm, turquoise bays.

Where to sail to next? Love in many ways is the simplest of things and then again it can get so obscured. How strange that at times it can feel its way as such a strong force and then be something that can wane away, grow pale and die. Does real love really die? I say no: I say you may not feel its force in your daily world, but there it lies and shall shock you or sooth you when it rises out of the past and introduces itself to you again.

So to those friends and lovers who have titled me that way in the past, then moved on, don't think that you don't live on in my heart, in some semblance; and never, ever imagine that you have left me for good. Real love doesn't work that way, that love is alive, though it may be dormant, even when its object is on a distant unseen horizon. And I understand you may say you love that thing, that one, no more, and still I reply that love changes, transmutes, shifts and transforms and can hide, but is always there, around and in you. Love is what makes you, love can guard you, buoy you; and when you think you lack love – you shrivel, you shrive and you waste.

If then you appreciate love in all its forms and not only the romantic him/her version – your world expands; the frequency of love letters coming to you pulses and increases and comes to you often and more – so much more when you choose to see it, in all its every glory. Quite simply – like attracts love… and so this letter ends….

With love, love, love…

From Me xxx

Letter to Gill Potter, at the Launch of her Book 'Sacred Paths Entwined'

Dear Gill

So many emotions gathered together as I shared your book launch with you... joy... pride... excitement... and more...

Here follows what is both a Love Letter to your book and a version of the speech, in 'real time' that I gave that evening in Glasgow, Scotland...

Welcome everyone to the launch of Gill's book 'Sacred Paths Entwined'. It is my joy and privilege to introduce you to both the author and the book.

Now I have a habit of writing love letters to life: to analyse, celebrate and give gratitude for the most inspirational and amazing things in my life and *this* is my love letter to Gill and her book...

This evening is a beginning, in so many ways... Of many new chapters, of lives changed, of destinies realised and released. The first of many new creations, of new connections, of lives changed inexorably and forever – starting here in this sacred space; this delicious pre-ordained bringing together of all of us, on this night of nights.

So... *Sacred Paths Entwined*... The very thing that brings us all together – to our destiny, and soul to soul – whether the reasons be known or unknown, through kin, friendship or fate... We might say in the grand scheme of things, that all these are one and the same – when we see, know and understand the phenomena, the very formula, of *Sacred Paths Entwined*.

That I am here with all of you tonight in this room, is, most definitely, a step on my own sacred path. That Gill and I are in each other's lives, is to us, no singular or random coincidence; it is a step on a sacred path, a joining together – for many reasons, brought together as we are by many golden connections and coincidences, and for reasons constantly revealed to us and yet, not yet all known to us still. Sacred paths entwined…

Now in terms of earthly time and space, ours is a short acquaintance, yet it is one packed with so much meaning for us… at a time of great transitions and steppings up and steppings out, in our separate and in our twinned lives.

In *my* working life, I am many things that you may recognise the labels of… I am leader, coach, entrepreneur, mentor, trainer and latterly too, also walking the path of author. Yet I am so many other characteristics, skills, aptitudes and stories too; and that is the glorious complexity of all of our lives and *'Sacred Paths Entwined'* reveals how all these should and could come together if we have the knowledge and the courage to follow our own sacred path.

So… here we are – Gillian and Sandra… how did we two souls come together in earthly ways? Although I live in the centre of England, we actually met here in

Scotland, in Edinburgh in fact, around about a year or so ago, at a 'Damsels in Success' event. Damsels is a women's self-development community that had just launched on an unsuspecting Scotland. As a leader in that sisterhood, I was there to support the start of a new group and Gill was there to find out more… She was following a calling as it happens, and also her natural, questing curiosity; and so it was that I found myself at her elbow – whispering and laughing and coaching and gently cajoling her to come and join the community of which I was a part. And so it was that we became sister members of the Damsels in Success community. She in Scotland, and me, still way back down south in Sassenach land.

And we didn't meet or connect again until many months later… I'm vague on all the timings and facts, whereas Gill will relate and remember them all with perfect memory and detail… As she is an astrologer and aligned as they are in the stars and in our traversing of this particular planet.

So, now, moving on through time and happenstance, we had moved from being distant sister members of Damsels in Success, to becoming sister *leaders*, each of our own groups.

So, as the first ever appointed Damsels leader, I was asked by Lucie Bradbury, Founder of Damsels in Success, to be Gill's mentor – to support and coach her, to care for in her new leadership role. Gill told me early on that I went above and beyond the job description, yet we realised as we travelled our piece of the path together, that it has been my calling to be who I am in her life story and what I am to her and she has always rewarded me, in so many ways, for the things that I have given, even though at times it does not seem like a fair exchange, yet we know that all will be balanced some where along our sacred paths entwined.

And it has been a truly gorgeous and ripe association… I have had the joy and the privilege of supporting her and encouraging her and answering her questions and listening to her learnings and her loathings and her lovings – walking with her on this living path, in this earthly plane of being, off and on, from where we met, to where we are now and of course, onwards into our futures. And as is the way the universe works, it was pre-ordained for us, that mentor becomes mentored, becomes gifted with the talents of her loving charge and becomes friend. Sacred paths entwined.

Gill came into my orbit, has spent time in my home and in my heart, as a sister spirit. Now Gill is a friend to me, a guide to me, an inspiration to me and so so many other things… And she has given me one of her greatest gifts – to cast my own *'Sacred Contract'* with her. So it was time for me – to reveal and then to activate my own contract: my divinely pre-ordained purpose, to be shown to and shared with the world. Elucidating my qualities and my character, understanding my traits and my trials. Shining the light on my own shining being and opening myself out to be my purpose, to live the dreams I was born with and nurtured for and so secretly harboured, as they were part of my soul, my life, my very love. Sacred paths entwined.

And Damsels in Success was the vehicle that bought us together and was the catalyst for so many things and still so it was that other things were in the universal store for Gill and she passed the leadership of her gorgeous Glasgow group to me, as it became so clear that her own shining purpose was finding yet another alchemical way of becoming breath, of becoming book: *Sacred Paths Entwined*. This book wherein lies the golden threads of her life, her purpose, her god-given gifts, her life's learnings: all bound together, all encapsulated to share, to bare, to teach, to inspire. Sacred paths entwined.

With this book share Gill's story, see who *you* are in the stars; learn yourself, know how to cast your contract and live your joyful purpose. It is all here in these pages, in Gill's magnum opus – which is, quite literally, and in every way, her true life's work!'

And this was our story – till now and this is a *Love Letter to Gill* and to her book, now born into the world.

With much love

Sandie xx

Gill and I celebrate 'Sacred Paths Entwined'

Letter to Life

Dear Life

Wow... Dear Life ... this is a big one ... Where on earth do I start?

Before there was time: you know how it was dear friend ... Out there in the ether of pre-existence, in the soul space before breath ... I actually *asked* to be born ... Oh me – me – *me* – please! Give me this; I want to be this; to experience physical life...

So the request was granted and the body was created and the baby born into this physical world, this earthbound entity that holds me with gravity to it: sometimes solidly, sometimes swaying and yes... sometimes staggering...

Life ... huge yet so narrow too... social and egotistical; unknown yet partly predictable; peculiar and of course, for me – Peachey.

Thank you my friend for this gift, for creating this one spark of nature, this animate, sentient creature. A unique creation from a billion strands of DNA, from how many millions of ancestors, linked and paired and then mutated to me.

Oh Life... how strange it is to think that this physicality is temporary – that very knowing has terrified me so much, so often... yet it is this *same* fact that makes you so very precious too. And here I am living and breathing, and yet *you* know that so often I have wished that I had never been born ... There have been times of tears when the fear and the pain and more failure and the knowledge of death, made me wish I never was ... Yet then too how can I now even conceive of *not* being – that is a really tough insanity, such a weird dichotomy.

So, my thoughts and feelings ebb and flow: from fear, to joy, to acceptance, to peaceful surrender.

So I love and I explore and I celebrate the light of living. And your most treasured gift to me dear Life – is *love*. It drives me, it defines me, it is an interlocked element of the air that I inhale and exhale; the air that I fly on, yes and the air that I *rock* with.

Having been given this diaphanous gift of life, I must remember, so often to actually *live* it. For there have been times when I have merely existed... been a crawling shell of necessity, simply functioning to survive ... *Survive* – what a crazy luxury to state! When I live within the comfortable parameters of easy, modern, western world living: with food, with shelter and of course with love. Still, many of us simply *exist* within these parameters don't we? We eat, sleep, fill our time (with work or chores or friends) and dull the pain. Then we wake up and do it all again tomorrow. Yet there is a choice. In *this* Peachey world there *is* a choice: in this head, in this heart there are internal alternatives to mere existence. And so many people are not aware that this choice is here... Most are 'presented' with life and get on with it – playing with the pack of cards life has dealt. Some say it is *all* about choice and

how we react. I say life *does* deal its pack, there is
no doubt of that... (Did I *ask* for blue eyes and to
be born in England for example? I don't remember
asking for those!) Still, when there is choice, we can
find the ace, produce a flush – not just a flash in the
pan.

How can we literally live life to the full? How is it
possible to be the genuinely grateful recipients of
this greatest of gifts? Every one of us is a special
composition – a one-off symphony of nature,
nurture, learning, and skills... You can only be
you, so start there... What defines you? What is
your flavour, your hue? Never tell me you have
nothing – no! Now – map, then travel through your
characteristics... Where do these fit into the grand
scheme of your being; how does this interlock with
those around you? Do you have the right cast with
you on your stage? Are you seriously supported??
How does your 'flavour', your magic uniqueness
match your environment? Are you in the right
place? Inside *and* out?

How does all that look, sound and smell to you?
How does that *feel*? Is it right? Or wrong? A mixture
of the two? Dare to consider it... This is *your* life
after all. *Your* gift: in your hands. *Never* think it all
rests in someone else's hands! Don't blame or claim
it is someone else's doing. These are your thoughts
and feelings, they are *your* dreams and desires...
And I know so many of us crave the 'outside': the
wealth, the things, the happenings that will make it
all all right... Yes I know, only too well... Yet it is all

nothing, if *inside* is not a match, if your soul is not reconciled – if it is angry, is waiting, is wanting...

Then it becomes time to decide and to take action... Not just once of course – for most of us, there are different directions to move in, at different times in our gift of life. So what *is* the answer then? Well, that is for *you* to know, to be guided to. Every one of us has our own path to take, so there is not a one size fits all solution. Ah – 'guided' – how glib, how easy for *me* to say! I say – get the guidance: follow your heart, then ask, read, research, find mentors, like-minded lifers. Invest in yourself – your time, your energy and your commitment to *living*, not being. Respect and honour and treasure this *gift* you have been given.

Dear Life... Time now to climb off my soapbox – the passion of my feeling for you, scares and stirs and enervates me!

Then this is my love letter to you dear friend: small and awesome, meandering and meaningful. Changing pace, constricting and contracting, just as you do. Herein is the complication of life, the simplification of life, contained in the creation of this – my letter, with a life of its own.

So there I end, with much love, to you – *always*.

Sandra

CHAPTER 9
My Peachey Conclusion

Me, being a dancing queen:
the Women Inspiring Women Awards,
sponsored by Damsels in Success. June 2012

Letter to Fruition

Dear Fruition

So there you are – that is you and my words together; and now it is time to slow the flow to a finish, to its own fantastic fruition.

Together we have streamed from seeing the seed within and then contemplated its stone. On then we pushed through the flesh to peel the skin and feel over its fuzz. Soon it was time to sample the fruit and thence from this fruition, so to reap the harvest. To harvest is to get all you can from the fruit – to squeeze the juice out of the peach, to eat, to slake and to quench. After this it was time to climb the tree, to know it and to contemplate it, and finally to sit in its shade. Time to see the sun, feel the possibility of oncoming rain and to completely appreciate the natural unhurried beauty of the orchard we inhabit.

This is a mere portion of a Peachey life, served up to you, and all for me. And all for you too: to take what you will from this Peachey piece of creation. I crave your intelligent indulgence as I have danced with my demons, given gratitude for my gathered gifts and worked through my Peachey stuff. Here is a life in letters – containing issues seen, shared, touched, heard, thought, felt and tasted, a full symphony of the senses, playing itself out, to its own melody of changing beat and tempo.

This book is the fruit that must now be gathered from the tree. Maybe it will fall. Maybe it will be carefully garnished and collected, taken to the market stall of the world, to be passed by or pounced upon.

Here of course I set *my* stall and put my book on it – sending my *Peachey Letters* out into the ether: to touch, to connect, to change, to entertain, to occupy and so to coach. They have coached and changed me, these letters of mine, and it is my wish that you are coached too, to verity, to freedom, to laughter, to release. They are here so you know that you are not alone, in who you are, in what you do and how you 'be'. I share my wares to show the ways that have worked for me – to release, to explore, to understand and to appreciate being *Peachey* and being whatever being Peachey is for *you*.

I have shaken the tree, harvested and explored the fruit, in all its boundless roundness, and now I shall love it and let it go. To sow the next seeds, some with purpose, others randomly scattered. I wonder where the next tree will be? I wonder what will come back to me?

Many have told me that they have now been inspired to write their own love letters to loved ones and to life. If *you* are called to do this, follow your instinct and remember that the key to coaching yourself here is to explore, understand and to give gratitude. This is vital – to raise your vibration and go beyond sharing your feelings and getting things off your chest. The process of celebration expands, it heals, it weaves its own coaching magic. Having written your letter or letters, decide to keep the letters to yourself or to go public (with one or with many) –

do what feels right for you. These are your products, your thoughts and feelings – let them go where they need to, and so if their purpose is to stay on the page or be seen by others – either purpose works in its place. If you are unsure how to play this, maybe there is one trusted person you can show them to first, someone who can see into you, can let you know how to proceed.

I know I was scared to share my first letters, it felt like a self-serving, public indulgence – yet *still* I published my blog. I was impelled to it, the idea came to me and the letters simply had to be. In fact – in truth, I cringed when I finally pushed the button that published the first letter on the world wide web. I made that move at bedtime at the end of one long day, only to be astonished the next morning by an amazing, positive and emotional reaction from a whole plethora of people; and so, it was that the beginnings of my book were born.

Here then were my *Peachey Letters*. Learn what you will from them, love what you will, enjoy, grow and gain from what ever nurtures you, and if it is *this* peach that feeds you, then that is as it is. Whatever you have got, thank you for being on this page, and may *your* life always be Peachey too.

With love and gratitude

From me to you, xx

Sandra Peachey - Author.

And that's me – Sandra Peachey

Praise for 'Peachey Letters ~ Love Letters to Life'

I love, love, love your book... you are such a talented and humorous writer, the combination of which make your book such an enjoyable and delightful read... You have given birth to a beautiful unique gift... it now has its own journey to take and who knows which people's lives it will touch...

~ Liz Ivory – Co Founder of Broadband Consciousness

Sandra Peachey has produced a fascinating book of heartfelt letters... As a reader it invokes a desire to start writing my own letters to experience the flow of exploration and insight, as well as drawing together my own life story... Congratulations to Sandra for a heartfelt, moving and insightful read.

~ Sue Maggott – 'Inspirational Poetry'

A M A Z I N G... this is such a wonderful, moving, heartfelt read, it is absolutely compelling. What I love about it most is your raw honesty and how I was able to relate to so much of what you describe... Your ability to communicate what you feel and who you really are is wonderful... You convey so much about the artist you are – beautifully creative, sensitive, a deep thinker and a beautiful soul that cares so much about life and the people in it. AWESOME, truly AWESOME.

~ Sarah Christie – Owner, 'Effective Outcomes'

Oh my – for me it's the 'Letter To The Juice'. Joyful Juicing and bellissimo Bellinis! Wonderful 'bespoke cocktail' and setting delicious Peachey intentions. Mmmm, my mouth waters and spirit wants to drink up her fill! Thank you Sandie, simply beautiful and mouth wateringly wonderful.

~ Lynn Burns – Founder of 'Suddenly Single Money'

An amazing book in which Sandra shares her thoughts and feelings in a way that will touch so many. Heartfelt and inspiring – a book that helps us think about what we have, what we want and what's truly important in our lives. Beautifully crafted – this book will help you not only learn more about Sandra, but also more about yourself. You'll laugh, cry, learn and be entertained.

~ Susan Brookes-Morris

I found the book brave and liberating and it has certainly made me feel grateful and reflective of all in my life past, present and future. Also, in such an instant, technological, fast moving, instant gratification, social media dominated society – the power of a letter has never been so strong as after reading your book.

~ Tara Fennessy

The book is a lovely gift to yourself or for a friend to share, in many of life's highs and lows, all with a modern twist! Sandra weaves her magic spell and takes you on an emotional journey to release joy and tears in equal measures while you read her delicious letters. Be prepared to open your heart (have tissues by your side) as you make each rite of passage with her and enjoy the surprises along the way!

~ Gill Potter – Author of *Sacred Paths Entwined*
www.joyfulsteps.com

It is delightful, especially from an autobiographical standpoint, and the pictures make it fun too! What a great idea for a book – letters. I really appreciated the personal ones to your mother and father, and to love... This is YOUR song and it is lovely.

~ Gigi Delmonico

Written with aching honesty and uncontrived eloquence, Sandra Peachey has beautifully captured the art of questioning, understanding and appreciating our journey through this thing we call life.

~ Isabel Gainford – Visual and Verbal Branding Specialist

Your book is phenomenal. I'm so jealous that I didn't write it! It has every ingredient for success and I felt just about every emotion there is on reading it.

~ Janice Bradbury

ABOUT THE AUTHOR

SANDRA PEACHEY is many things… including an entrepreneur, and with her own business – 'Peachey Days', she coaches, trains and mentors – working with corporate clients, small businesses, job seekers and individual 'life seekers'. Her role is to guide and support the attainment of dreams and goals, using a range of practical and inspirational tools and techniques. This in turn provides the freedom for 'seekers' everywhere to choose the life they live, and make the most of the life they choose.

Contact her at: info@peachey-days.co.uk

Website: www.peacheydays.co.uk

Printed in Great Britain
by Amazon.co.uk, Ltd.,
Marston Gate.